MEDICAL
EVALUATION
OF PHYSICALLY
AND
SEXUALLY
ABUSED
CHILDREN

THE APSAC STUDY GUIDES 3

The APSAC Study Guides

Jon R. Conte, Series Editor

The APSAC Study Guides are intended to provide an outline of critical knowledge in selected aspects of child maltreatment and to direct the reader to important research and other knowledge. Prepared by leading experts in each area, the study guides offer these experts' summaries of important knowledge areas, some critical analysis of the knowledge and issues in each area, and the identification of critical questions raised by the knowledge in the particular area of child maltreatment.

In this series:

Founded in 1987, the American Professional Society on the Abuse of Children (APSAC) is the nation's largest interdisciplinary professional society for those working in the field of child abuse and neglect. APSAC's mission is to improve society's response to the abuse and neglect of its children by promoting effective interdisciplinary approaches to the identification, intervention, treatment, and prevention of child maltreatment.

APSAC

American Professional Society on the Abuse of Children
407 S. Dearborn, Suite 1300
Chicago, IL 60605
Phone: 312-554-0166
Fax: 312-554-0919

CAROLE
JENNY

MEDICAL
EVALUATION
OF PHYSICALLY
AND
SEXUALLY
ABUSED
CHILDREN

THE APSAC STUDY GUIDES 3

Published in cooperation with the
American Professional Society
on the Abuse of Children

SAGE Publications
International Educational and Professional Publisher
Thousand Oaks   London   New Delhi

For information address:

SAGE Publications, Inc.
2455 Teller Road
Thousand Oaks, California 91320
E-mail: order@sagepub.com

SAGE Publications Ltd.
6 Bonhill Street
London EC2A 4PU
United Kingdom

SAGE Publications India Pvt. Ltd.
M-32 Market
Greater Kailash I
New Delhi 110 048 India

Printed in the United States of America

Library of Congress Cataloging-in-Publication Data

Jenny, Carole.
    Medical evaluation of physically and sexually abused children / author, Carole Jenny.
        p.   cm. — (APSAC study guides)
    Includes bibliographical references.
    ISBN 0-7619-0397-6
    1. Battered child syndrome—Diagnosis. 2. Sexually abused children—Medical examinations.   I. Title. II. Series.
RA1122.5.J46 1996
618.92′858223—dc20   96-4507

96 97 98 99 10 9 8 7 6 5 4 3 2 1
This book is printed on acid-free paper.
Sage Production Editor: Diana E. Axelsen
Sage Typesetter: Danielle Dillahunt
Cover Designer: Dawn Anderson

Contents

Series Editor's Introduction

The APSAC Study Guides were born out of the ongoing commitment of the American Professional Society on the Abuse of Children (APSAC) to provide the latest information, current knowledge, and best ideas about practice to its members and other professionals who work in child maltreatment.

The guides are intended to provide an outline of critical knowledge in selected aspects of child maltreatment and to direct the reader to important research and other knowledge. Prepared by leading experts in each area, the study guides offer these experts' summaries of important knowledge areas, some critical analysis of the knowledge and issues in each area, and the identification of critical questions raised by the knowledge in the particular area of child maltreatment.

It is important to bear in mind what the study guides are not. They are not intended to be a full summary of critical knowledge, research knowledge, or critical analyses of professional research and knowledge. They are not intended to remove the need of the professional to keep current in research and other professional literatures. Neither the guides nor the knowledge tests available from PsychoEducational Resources are intended to be a process for the certification of professionals, knowledge, or specific aspects of practice.

The guides can serve as road maps to important papers, chapters, and articles that readers can obtain in order to pursue topics and explore perspectives. The reader is encouraged to use the study guide as one source for critical comments and points of view about this literature and to see how the reader's own ideas, analysis, or opinions agree or disagree with those of the study guide author.

Knowledge testing is made possible through collaboration with PsychoEducational Resources (PER). The knowledge test, client vignette questions, and related materials are located in a perforated section at the end of the book. Tear out this section, complete the test questions, sign the form verifying your completion of this home study program, complete the program evaluation/participant satisfaction form, and mail these materials to:

PsychoEducational Resources
P. O. Box 2196
Keystone Heights, FL 32656

If you have questions regarding the testing or the awarding of CE credits, call PER at (904) 473-7300.

PER is approved by the American Psychological Association to offer continuing education for psychologists and by the Florida Board of Licensed Clinical Social Work, Marriage and Family Therapy, and Mental Health Counseling (CM #406, '97). PER is also approved by the Connecticut chapter of NASW, and it conforms to the standards of the following states for awarding CE credits to social workers: Alabama, Arkansas, Georgia, Idaho, Kansas, Nebraska, New Hampshire, New Mexico, Oregon, Texas, and West Virginia. These CE sponsorships are honored by many state boards of social work, marriage and family therapy, and professional counseling. Other state approvals are pending. Some restrictions may apply. Check with your state board or call PER at the number above. PER maintains responsibility for these programs and adheres to all sponsorship guidelines for providing CE credits.

Be aware that the knowledge test includes some questions from the key literature to which you are guided in the manual. Six CE credits are awarded with an 80% pass on the tests. Quizzes may be retaken without penalty or additional charge if the pass rate is not met initially. The cost of testing and awarding of CE credit and certificate is included in the price of the book.

APSAC is the nation's largest interdisciplinary society for professionals working in the field of child abuse and neglect. One of APSAC's primary aims is to ensure that everyone affected by child maltreatment receives the best possible professional response. To that end, APSAC produces a wide range of professional publications, including the quarterly journal, *Child Maltreatment*; the quarterly newsletter, *The APSAC Advisor*; guidelines for interdisciplinary professional practice; and *The APSAC Handbook on Child Maltreatment*. The APSAC Study Guides series is yet another important avenue through which APSAC seeks to implement its commitment to ongoing professional education.

JON R. CONTE
University of Washington

Acknowledgments

The author wishes to thank the past and current physician members of the APSAC Board of Directors who took time to review the manuscript, including Robert Reece, M.D., Howard Dubowitz, M.D., Paula Jaudes, M.D., Carolyn Levitt, M.D., Astrid Heger, M.D., David Chadwick, M.D., Randall Alexander, M.D., and Martin Finkel, D.O. I am also thankful to the series editor, Jon Conte, Ph.D., for his patience.

Introduction

This APSAC Study Guide has been designed to introduce the reader to the current spectrum of knowledge contained in the medical literature about the physical and sexual abuse of children. It is *not* meant to be a textbook on child abuse, but rather to serve as a "road map" to guide the reader to the best available information and to help them to find that information in the vast medical literature. There are no photographs or illustrations in the body of the text of this book.

To make the study guide more accessible to the non-medical reader, a glossary of medical terms is provided in the last chapter. The definitions included are in layperson's terms.

Each chapter begins with a list of basic references. The articles and textbooks in each list constitute the basic resources a person working in the field would want to have readily at hand. A discussion of the basic knowledge in the field follows, with extensive references at the end of each chapter for the reader to find a more thorough discussion of the topic. Most of the references at the end of the chapters will be found in a well-stocked medical library. In addition, online reference retrieval services are offered through the Internet where articles can be ordered. In areas where controversy exists, articles on both sides of the issue are referenced.

Objectives

A. To acquaint the reader with the substantive areas that are fundamental to the evaluation of *physical* abuse. Knowledge areas to be covered include the following:

1. Epidemiology and risk factors of physical abuse

2. Main features distinguishing physical abuse from accidental injury

3. Principles of interviewing children and adults about suspected abuse

4. Basic information that is gathered by law enforcement and social services personnel at a crime scene investigation

5. Components of a complete physical examination in child abuse cases

6. Requirements for accurate and usable photodocumentation of abuse-related injuries

7. Appropriate use of laboratory and radiological tests to evaluate suspected abuse, including skeletal surveys, bone scans, computerized tomography, magnetic resonance imagery, ultrasonography, blood counts and urinalyses, clotting studies, liver function studies, and serum amylase

8. Legal requirements for chart documentation in child abuse cases

9. Presentation of and tests needed for diagnosis of intra-abdominal trauma resulting from child abuse

10. Types and patterns of burns more likely to be associated with child abuse

11. Thirteen characteristics of burn cases that increase the likelihood that the burn was a result of abuse

12. Presentation of intrathoracic trauma resulting from child abuse

13. Identification of common patterns of injury inflicted to the face, ears, mouth, nose, and throat of abused children

14. Common patterns of fractures found in child abuse

15. Stages of healing seen in bone injuries

16. Identification of diseases that can cause pathological fractures resembling those found in abused children

17. Common patterns of head injuries found in child abuse

18. Spectrum of eye injuries found in child abuse

19. Differential diagnosis of retinal hemorrhages

20. Common "pattern injuries" that occur in abused children, based on the object with which the child was hit

21. Patterns and numbers of bruises that occur commonly on non-abused children based on age and developmental level

B. To acquaint the reader with the substantive areas that are fundamental to the evaluation of *sexual* abuse. Knowledge areas to be covered include the following:

1. Epidemiology of and risk factors for sexual abuse

2. Signs and symptoms of sexual abuse of children

3. Psychological effect of sexual abuse on children

4. Principles of interviewing children in a medical setting for suspected sexual abuse

5. Techniques for physical examination of the genitalia and anus in cases of suspected child sexual abuse

6. Indications for internal speculum and bimanual examinations.

7. Identification of normal physical findings in anal and genital examinations

8. Effect of normal development on the genitalia of children

9. Identification of normal anatomic variants, pathologic conditions, and conditions resulting from trauma unrelated to but commonly confused with sexual abuse

10. Common physical findings of the genitalia and anus related to acute, sub-acute, and healed (sexual abuse) trauma

11. Changes in sexual abuse trauma that occur with healing over time

12. Identification of the advantages and disadvantages of using the photo-colposcope and other methods of documentation in the examination of sexually abused children and adolescents

13. Principles of forensic examination and specimen collection after acute sexual assault

14. Basic scientific principles underlying the application of forensic micros-copy, serology, and biochemistry in sexual assault cases

15. Legal requirements for chart documentation in child sexual abuse cases

16. Common non-venereal pathogens and conditions causing vulvitis, vaginitis, and anal infections in children

17. Epidemiology, modes of transmission, and legal implications of common sexually transmitted pathogens in children

18. Diagnostic tests for sexually transmitted and associated microorganisms in children

Child Physical Abuse

Epidemiology, Risk Factors, and Evaluation

Basic References

Jenny, C., & Hay, T. C. (1994). *The visual diagnosis of child physical abuse.* Elk Grove Village, IL: American Academy of Pediatrics.

This is a collection of 150 slides submitted by members of the American Academy of Pediatrics. It includes a teaching text explaining each slide. The slides represent many of the visual findings in child abuse cases, including radiologic images.

Helfer, R. E., & Kempe, R. S. (1987). *The battered child* (4th ed.). Chicago: University of Chicago Press.

This book covers psychological, medical, and legal aspects of abuse. It is considered to be a classic in the field. A new edition is in press but is not yet available.

Reece, R. M. (1994). *Child abuse: Medical diagnosis and management.* Philadelphia: Lea & Febiger.

This text reviews the entire field of child abuse. It is one of the most complete references available.

Discussion

Child abuse reports to social service agencies increased 40% nationwide between 1985 and 1991. In 1991, 2,694,000 child abuse and neglect reports were made. Of these reported cases, 25% involved allegations of physical abuse. Reports of abuse and neglect in day care or foster care accounted for less than 1% of total reports (Daro & McCurdy, 1992).

In 1991, 1,033 child abuse fatalities were reported. The rate most commonly accepted is about 2,000 deaths due to child abuse per year (U.S. Advisory Board on Child Abuse and Neglect, 1995). From 1985 to 1991, the rate of child abuse fatalities increased from 1.4 to 2.15 per 100,000 children, a 54% rise. Of the children who died from abuse or neglect between 1989 and 1991, 39% had prior or current contact with child protective service agencies. Of these victims, 54% were under 1 year old, and 79% were less than 5 years old (Daro & McCurdy, 1992).

Estimates of the percentage of injuries seen in emergency facilities resulting from child abuse vary from 1.3% to 15% (Pless, Sibald, Smith, & Russell, 1987). Variations in the prevalence of abusive injury from one community to another may result in these disparate figures.

Several risk factors for abusive injury have been identified. Male and minority children are at greater risk (Johnson & Showers, 1985), as well as children with low Apgar scores at birth, low birth weight (Goldson, Michael, Fitch, Wendell, & Knapp, 1978), and lower developmental quotients on standardized tests. Social isolation of families, urban location, low levels of maternal education, less skilled jobs held by mothers, unemployment, and poverty have been correlated with the occurrence of physical abuse (Jason, Williams, Burton, & Rochat, 1982; Krugman, Lenherr, Betz, & Fryer, 1986; Newberger, Hampton, Marx, & White, 1986). Also, families where the mother is single, separated, or divorced are at a higher risk. Other studies have not shown that the loss of a job in an otherwise stable family increases that risk (Taitz, King, Nicholson, & Kessel, 1987).

Several factors have been commonly identified as associated with cases of child abuse (Krugman, 1984; Valman, 1987), including the following:

1. *Discrepant history.* The history given by the caretakers does not account for the severity of the injury.

2. *Unreasonable delay in seeking care.* The delay will often adversely affect the child's outcome, especially after severe head or abdominal injuries.

3. *Inappropriate affect of caretakers.* Parents or guardians may not seem appropriately concerned about the nature and severity of injuries.

4. *Changing history.* Caretakers may prevaricate about the cause of injuries and continue to change the description of how the injury occurred, as they sense that the history they are giving is not an acceptable explanation of the injury.

5. *Patterns of injury commonly seen in child abuse.* Several common patterns of injury are known to be associated with abuse, including metaphyseal fractures, immersion burns, and shaken baby syndrome. Although abuse can cause a wide variety of injuries, some injuries are very uncommon if abuse has not occurred.

Other factors that have been identified with child abuse cases are the following:

1. *A family crisis.* A family may have unusual or traumatic stress shortly before abuse occurs.

2. *A trigger event preceding the abuse.* Some abuse may be in response to inconsolable infant crying, feeding difficulties, or toileting accidents.

3. *Unrealistic expectations.* Parents may be frustrated by expecting more from their children than the children can accomplish developmentally. Unrealistic expectations can precipitate anger from parents or guardians.

4. *Parents abused as children.* Although many adults abused as children grow up to be loving, caring adults, most abusive parents will have had physical or sexual abuse experiences as children.

It is important to remember that some abusive parents or caretakers will not fit the profile listed above. Also, some parents with many of the above characteristics will not be abusive. Each case needs to be carefully and individually evaluated.

STUDY QUESTIONS

1. What is the epidemiology of child physical abuse?
2. What risk factors have been identified for child physical abuse?
3. What are the main features that distinguish child physical abuse from accidental injury?

MEDICAL HISTORY

The role of the medical history in the investigation of cases of suspected child abuse is controversial. Physicians use the medical history to obtain information for diagnosis and treatment. The focus and content of the medical interview is quite different from that required by law enforcement and social service agencies (Newberger, 1990). However, it is necessary to reach a diagnostic impression about whether or not the injuries involve nonaccidental trauma, requiring a complete social history and a detailed, minute-by-minute analysis of the events leading up to the injury.

The following components of the medical history are important to obtain (Newberger, 1990):

1. What events preceded the injury? Ask the child's caretakers to discuss in great detail exactly what happened in the hours prior to presenting the child for medical care. When did they first notice the child was injured? How did the child's symptoms develop? In what order? What was the timing of evolution of the symptoms? When did the child last have a normal meal? What did the child eat and how much?

2. Who had access to the child prior to the injury? Who was in the home? Who took care of the child? Who might have witnessed the event?

3. Was there a precipitating event prior to the injury? Sometimes, abuse occurs during frustrating episodes involving feeding, toileting, or diaper changes. Fights between the parents may also precipitate abusive actions toward the children.

4. What is the child's nature? Is the child colicky, difficult to care for, in a frustrating developmental stage? What is the nature of the relationship between caretakers and the child?

5. What kind of response did the caretakers make to the injuries? Did they attempt first aid or cardiac resuscitation? Did they seek care promptly or delay seeking care?

6. What is the child's past medical history? Have there been past serious injuries, a history of apnea, seizures, or vomiting? Was the child's birth complicated or difficult? Was the child ill in the neonatal period? Is the child immunized? Has the child received well-child care and regular physical checkups?

7. What is the child's developmental level? Is the child "age appropriate" or delayed? Is the child physically and mentally capable of the acts described by the family, for example, can the child roll over? Can he or she climb into a bathtub and turn on the water? Can he or she climb onto a high surface?

8. If the child is verbal, a history from the child can be most helpful and should be elicited. An experienced clinician who is comfortable with interviewing children can ask the child what happened and who hurt them. Ask the child about other forms of abuse, such as sexual or emotional abuse or neglect. Document the child's affect and record the child's language, using exact quotes in the chart. This should be done without the presence of a parent, if possible.

9. If other children observed the injury, they can often tell what they saw, either directly or through acting out the episode in their play. In addition, siblings and other children exposed to any potential violence should be examined for injury.

The family and social history includes the following:

1. What is the family constellation? Who lives in the home and how are they related? What is the family support system? What extended family members are involved in the life of the family?

2. What are the social stressors in the family, such as poverty, unemployment, trouble with the law, family conflicts, domestic violence, previous involvement with child protective services, drug or alcohol use, divorce or separation?

3. What were the parents' (caretakers') experiences as children? Do they have a history of physical or sexual abuse or family violence?

4. How do the parents discipline the child?

5. Are the parents appropriately concerned, given the nature and severity of the child's injury? Are their affects appropriate?

STUDY QUESTION

4. Why obtain the medical history? What are the important components of the medical history?

ROLE OF THE "CRIME SCENE INVESTIGATION"

Although not a usual part of the medical examination, a survey of the child's environment where the abuse or accident occurred is an important part of the data-gathering process (Mead, Balch, & Westgate, 1988; Wagner,

1986). The questions asked should be influenced by the nature of the injury. For example, if the child is burned by tap water, the water temperature should be accurately measured. How much torque is required to turn the water faucet handles? How high are the handles from the floor or from the tub bottom? How is the bathtub drain occluded and how difficult is this to accomplish?

For falls, the distance to the floor should be measured and the nature and hardness of the surface described. What objects are present in the room? How is furniture arranged? When a fall down steps is alleged, how steep are the stairs? What is covering the stair treads? If a walker is involved, are there any scrapes or dents on it?

Generally, look for stains from blood, vomitus, or spilled food in the child's environment. An assessment of the general organization and safety of the household can give information on the risks and stress present. The presence of pets, safety hazards, and health hazards should be noted.

In addition to examining the place where the abuse occurred, other eye-witnesses, such as neighbors or visitors, should be sought out and interviewed.

PHYSICAL EXAMINATION OF ABUSED CHILDREN

Many children who are physically abused may have also been sexually abused, neglected, or both. The physical examination should be done as soon as the child is medically stable and should include the following (Jenny & Hay, 1994; Schmitt, 1987):

Growth Parameters. Careful measurements of height, weight, and head circumference should be plotted on standard growth charts and compared to growth data obtained from the child's birth records and other medical records. Rapidly increasing head size can indicate the time of a head injury in an infant. Low weight or poor growth can indicate neglect or failure to thrive.

Head-to-Toe Physical Examination. Bruises, burns, abrasions, or skin lesions should be carefully documented, measured, and photographed, using a size and color standard in the field. Swab any bite marks with two saline-moistened cotton swabs. Air dry the swabs and freeze at a constant low temperature or give to the appropriate law enforcement agent immediately for delivery to a forensic laboratory.

Carefully examine the scalp for edema, bruises, or redness. In infants, check the fontanelle for fullness or tenseness.

When examining the ears, nose, and throat, look for bleeding, tears of the frenulum, bruising, or abrasions inside the lips or in the pharynx. The eyegrounds should be examined after dilating the pupils by the most experienced examiner available. Check for retinal or pre-retinal hemorrhages or for bleeding into the vitreous or anterior chamber of the eye. Perform a careful and complete neurological examination. Document the state of consciousness and score on the Glasgow coma scale, if indicated.

During the chest and abdominal exam, look for evidence of blunt injury, rib tenderness, lung contusions, or intra-abdominal injury, such as ruptured spleen or viscus, or duodenal hematomas. On the extremities, palpate the long bones and examine the joints for swelling and tenderness.

S T U D Y   Q U E S T I O N

5. What basic information should be gathered by law enforcement and social services personnel at a crime scene investigation?

Genital and Anal Exam for Signs of Sexual Mistreatment. Carefully inspect the genitalia and anus for bruising, bleeding, scarring, or discharge. The condition and configuration of the hymen and introitus should be noted.

Examination of Siblings and Other Children in the Household. Other children in the family may also be at risk for abuse. They should be interviewed and examined.

LABORATORY AND RADIOLOGICAL TESTS

In all children less than 2 years old where physical abuse is suspected, a skeletal survey to look for occult fractures is recommended by the American Academy of Pediatrics (1991). After age 2, skeletal surveys should be considered, depending on the facts of the case. In one retrospective study, 11.5% of skeletal surveys were positive (Ellerstein & Norris, 1984). After age 5, the skeletal survey is not likely to be helpful in an asymptomatic child (American Academy of Pediatrics, 1991).

An adequate skeletal survey includes separate exposures of anteroposterior views of the arms, forearms, hands, femurs, lower legs, and feet; lateral views of the axial skeleton, as well as frontal views in infants; and anteroposterior and lateral views of the skull (American Academy of Pediatrics, 1991).

Radionuclide bone scans have been shown to be highly sensitive in detecting abuse-related fractures (Jaudes, 1984), but the lack of specificity of positive findings limit their usefulness. Bone scans may not detect metaphyseal injuries and spinal injuries. Radionuclide bone scans can be a helpful supplement to the skeletal survey in cases where trauma is suspected but the skeletal survey is normal. The skeletal survey, however, is generally considered the primary tool for the diagnosis of child abuse-related skeletal trauma (American Academy of Pediatrics, 1991).

In children with head injuries, computerized tomography (CT) imaging will visualize acute injuries requiring treatment. However, magnetic resonance imaging (MRI) is more effective in dating subdural hematomas and will pick up lesions missed by CT imaging, particularly posterior fossa bleeding, cortical injuries, and white matter injuries (Alexander, Schor, & Smith, 1986; Sato et al., 1989). MRI is more likely to be helpful in detecting child abuse-related head injuries, except for subarachnoid hemorrhage (American Academy of Pediatrics, 1991).

CT imaging of suspected thoracic and abdominal trauma is superior to other imaging methods (Kirks, 1983). CT identifies lung injury, pleural injuries, and injuries to solid organs. In small children, ultrasound is also useful. Free fluid in the abdomen can be visualized, as well as retroperitoneal and abdominal hematomas.

The role of clotting studies can be both helpful and confusing (O'Hare & Eden, 1984). When children present with abnormal bruising and petechial skin lesions, a prothrombin time, partial thromboplastin time, a platelet count, and a bleeding time can rule out clotting disorders. After serious injuries such as head trauma, the clotting studies are often abnormal because of consumption of coagulation factors in response to the injury (Miner, Kaufman, Graham, Haar, & Gildenberg, 1982). Severe shock can also cause abnormal studies. In these cases, tests for diffuse intravascular coagulation and an analysis of specific clotting factors are helpful in ruling out coagulation disorders as a cause of the pathology rather than as a result.

Analyses of liver enzymes in cases of suspected nonaccidental trauma have led to the diagnosis of a surprisingly high rate of occult liver injury (Coant, Kornberg, Brody, & Edward-Holmes, 1992). Particularly, serum transaminase levels have been predictive of liver trauma.

CHART DOCUMENTATION

Solomons (1980) found that only 40% of charts at a university hospital contained accurate documentation in cases of burns, fractures, contusions, or intracranial injuries to determine whether or not child abuse had been considered. In this study, he used four criteria to determine chart adequacy. The charts needed to include a history of the injury, a description of the injury, documentation of previous injuries or accidents, and an analysis of whether or not the injury was consistent with the history given. A well-documented chart can make the job of a physician much easier when called to testify months or years after the injury.

An important part of documenting the chart is photodocumentation of injury. "A picture is worth a thousand words" is an adage that is extremely applicable to child abuse cases. Any medical facility caring for abused children needs to have a well-designed system for case documentation. An excellent review of photographic issues is found in Reece's text, *Child Abuse: Medical Diagnosis and Management* (Ricci, 1994).

STUDY QUESTIONS

6. What are the components of a complete physical examination in child abuse cases?

7. What are the requirements for accurate and usable photodocumentation of abuse-related injuries?

8. Describe the appropriate use of laboratory and radiological tests to evaluate suspected abuse, including skeletal surveys, bone scans, computerized tomography, magnetic resonance imagery, ultrasonography, blood counts and urinalyses, clotting studies, liver function studies, and serum amylase.

9. What are the legal requirements for chart documentation in child abuse cases?

SUMMARY

Medical personnel can offer important data to others investigating alleged physical child abuse. Coordination and cooperation are important for obtaining the most thorough and accurate assessment of the child's injuries.

References

Alexander, R. C., Schor, D. P., & Smith, W. L. (1986). Magnetic resonance imaging of intracranial injuries from child abuse. *Journal of Pediatrics, 109*, 975-979.

American Academy of Pediatrics, Section on Radiology. (1991). Diagnostic imaging of child abuse. *Pediatrics, 87*, 262-264.

Coant, P. N., Kornberg, A. E., Brody, A. S., & Edward-Holmes, K. (1992). Markers for occult liver injury in cases of physical abuse in children. *Pediatrics, 89*, 274-278.

Daro, D., & McCurdy, K. (1992). *Current trends in child abuse reporting and fatalities: The results of the 1991 annual Fifty-State Survey* (Working Paper No. 808). Chicago: National Center on Child Abuse Prevention Research.

Ellerstein, N. S., & Norris, K. J. (1984). Value of radiologic skeletal survey in assessment of abused children. *Pediatrics, 74*, 1075-1078.

Goldson, E., Michael, J., Fitch, M. J., Wendell, T. A., & Knapp, G. (1978). Child abuse: Its relationship to birthweight, Apgar scores, and developmental testing. *American Journal of Diseases of Children, 132*, 790-793.

Jason, J., Williams, S. L., Burton, A., & Rochat, R. (1982). Epidemiologic differences between sexual and physical child abuse. *JAMA, 247*, 3344-3348.

Jaudes, P. K. (1984). Comparison of radiography and radionuclide bone scanning in the detection of child abuse. *Pediatrics, 73*, 166-168.

Jenny, C., & Hay, T. C. (1994). *The visual diagnosis of child physical abuse.* Elk Grove Village, IL: American Academy of Pediatrics.

Johnson, C. F., & Showers, J. (1985). Injury variables in child abuse. *Child Abuse & Neglect, 9*, 207-215.

Kirks, D. R. (1983). Radiological evaluation of visceral injuries in the battered child syndrome. *Pediatric Annals, 12*, 888-893.

Krugman, R. D. (1984). Child abuse and neglect: The role of the primary care physician in recognition, treatment, and prevention. *Primary Care, 11*, 527-534.

Krugman, R. D., Lenherr, M., Betz, L., & Fryer, G. E. (1986). The relationship between unemployment and physical abuse of children. *Child Abuse & Neglect, 10*, 415-418.

Mead, J. J., Balch, G. M., & Westgate, D. L. (1988). *Investigating child abuse.* Brea, CA: RC Law & Co.

Miner, M. E., Kaufman, H. H., Graham, S. H., Haar, F. H., & Gildenberg, P. L. (1982). Disseminated intravascular coagulation fibrinolytic syndrome following head injury in children: Frequency and prognostic implications. *Journal of Pediatrics, 100*, 687-691.

Newberger, E. H. (1990). Pediatric interview assessment of child abuse. *Pediatric Clinics of North America, 37*, 943-954.

Newberger, E. H., Hampton, R. L., Marx, T. J., & White, K. M. (1986). Child abuse and pediatric social illness: An epidemiological analysis and ecological reformulation. *American Journal of Orthopsychiatry, 56*(4), 589-601.

O'Hare, A. E., & Eden, O. B. (1984). Bleeding disorders and non-accidental injury. *Archives of Diseases in Childhood, 59*, 860-864.

Pless, I. B., Sibald, A. D., Smith, M. A., & Russell, M. D. (1987). A reappraisal of the frequency of child abuse seen in pediatric emergency rooms. *Child Abuse & Neglect, 11*, 193-299.

Ricci, L. R. (1994). Photodocumentation of the abused child. In R. M. Reece (Ed.), *Child abuse: Medical diagnosis and management* (pp. 248-265). Philadelphia: Lea & Febiger.

Sato, Y., Yuh, W. T., Smith, W. L., Alexander, R. C., Kao, S. C., & Ellerbroek, C. J. (1989). Head injury in child abuse: Evaluation with MR imaging. *Radiology, 173,* 653-657.

Schmitt, B. D. (1987). The child with nonaccidental trauma. In R. E. Helfer & R. S. Kempe (Eds.), *The battered child* (pp. 178-198). Chicago: University of Chicago Press.

Solomons, G. (1980). Trauma and child abuse. *American Journal of Diseases of Children, 134,* 503-505.

Taitz, L. S., King, J. M., Nicholson, J., & Kessel, M. (1987). Unemployment and child abuse. *British Medical Journal (Clinical Research), 294,* 1074-1076.

U.S. Advisory Board on Child Abuse and Neglect. (1995). *A nation's shame: Fatal child abuse and neglect in the United States.* Washington, DC: Department of Health and Human Services, Administration for Children and Families.

Valman, H. B. (1987). Child abuse. *British Medical Journal (Clinical Research), 294,* 633-635.

Wagner, G. N. (1986). Crime scene investigation in child-abuse cases. *American Journal of Forensic Medicine and Pathology, 7,* 94-99.

Abdominal Trauma

Basic References

Ledbetter, D. J., Hatch, E. I., Feldman, K. W., Fligner, C. L., & Tapper, D. (1988). Diagnostic and surgical implications of child abuse. *Archives of Surgery, 123,* 1101-1105.

This article reviews 8 years of experience with abusive abdominal injuries in children at two urban hospitals. The types of injuries encountered are described and compared with accidental trauma.

Kirks, D. R. (1983). Radiological evaluation of visceral injuries in the battered child syndrome. *Pediatric Annals, 12,* 888-893.

This article reviews not only radiologic issues in diagnosis but pathophysiology as well.

Cooper, A., Floyd, T., Barlow, B., Niemirska, M., Ludwig, S., Seidl, T., O'Neill, J., Templeton, J., Ziegler, M., Ross, A., Gandhi, R., &

Catherman, R. (1988). Major blunt abdominal trauma due to child abuse. *Journal of Trauma, 28,* 1483-1486.

The authors emphasize the complications that occur when children present with abusive injuries but no history of injury. They also review the mortality of abuse cases.

DiMaio, D. J., & DiMaio, V. J. M. (1989). *Forensic Pathology* (pp. 122-132). New York: Elsevier.

Although not specifically about children, the chapter in this text on abdominal injuries provides a wealth of information about the mechanism of injury and types of trauma affecting the abdomen.

Coant, P. N., Kornberg, A. E., Brody, A. S., & Edward-Holmes, K. (1992). Markers for occult liver injury in cases of physical abuse in children. *Pediatrics, 89,* 274-278.

The authors report an elegantly done study that serves as an example of quality clinical research.

Discussion

Although not common, abusive abdominal injuries to children carry a mortality rate of about 50% (Cooper et al., 1988). They are more commonly fatal than accidental abdominal injuries (Ledbetter, Hatch, Feldman, Fligner, & Tapper, 1988), probably because of the delay in seeking care and because a history of injury is not presented to the treatment team.

Children are more susceptible to abdominal trauma than adults. Their abdominal muscles are relatively weak, and their rib cages cover less of the upper abdomen, leaving the liver and upper abdominal structures exposed. They have shorter anterior-posterior diameters to their trunks, making forces from blows more likely to extend to the posterior abdominal wall (Cooper, 1992).

Penetrating abdominal trauma is rarely reported in child abuse cases. With blunt abdominal trauma, two basic mechanisms of abdominal injury occur (Kirks, 1983). Compression, crushing, or squeezing can cause rupture of the solid organs or hollow organs. Intestinal rupture from compression trauma is more likely to occur on the surface opposite the attachment of the mesentery. More commonly, deceleration forces from direct blows, kicks, or falls against objects cause internal injuries. With deceleration forces, intestinal injury often occurs at the site of ligamentous support or immobilization or at the site of compression of the internal organs against the spine. In either case, serious intra-abdominal injury often occurs without any external bruising or trauma noted on the abdomen (Kleinman, Raptopoulos, & Brill, 1981).

The distribution of types of abdominal injuries resulting from abuse differs from that resulting from accidental injury. Ledbetter et al. (1988) studied injuries seen over an 11-year period. They found that 65% of battered children with abdominal injuries had bowel injuries, whereas only 8% of children with accidental abdominal injuries had hollow viscus (stomach or bowel) injuries. For the accidental injury group, hollow viscus injuries occurred after high-energy impact, such as in automobile accidents. This implies that the forces sustained by abused children from direct abdominal blows far exceeds that which occurs in simple falls and common accidents.

Of the solid organs, the liver is the most likely to be injured in abusive trauma, followed by the pancreas as the next most common (Ledbetter et al., 1988). Injuries to the spleen and kidneys are uncommon in child abuse cases and much more likely to be due to accidental injury. One possible explanation is that child abuse injuries are more likely to be downward blows (from a taller person hitting or kicking a shorter person), which allows the rib cage to protect the spleen.

Discussions of individual types of abusive abdominal trauma follows.

Small Bowel Injuries. Although an uncommon injury, intramural small bowel hematomas are often the result of abuse (Jewett, Caldarola, Karp, Allen, & Cooney, 1988). Most will occur in the duodenum where the retroperitoneal portion affixes it to the posterior abdominal wall. Hematomas can also occur in the jejunum. The diagnosis can be difficult and symptoms nonspecific. Although most small intestine hematomas resolve spontaneously, they can rupture and cause exsanguination. Malnutrition and dehydration can occur from obstruction.

Although intraluminal hematomas have sometimes been diagnosed by ultrasound (Hermanz-Schulman & Genieser, 1989), upper gastrointestinal contrast studies are usually needed to diagnose the mass lesion (Suson, Klotz, & Kottmeier, 1975). The lesions may not be visualized on abdominal CT.

Small bowel perforations can also result from blunt abuse injuries (Cobb, Vinocur, Wagner, & Weintraub, 1986). Kleinman (1987) found 60% to occur in the jejunum, distal to the ligament of Treitz. Thirty percent are in the duodenum and 10% in the ileum. Bleeding or avulsion of the adjacent mesentery often occurs. Intraperitoneal perforations usually produce dramatic symptoms of abdominal discomfort, although the development of symptoms may be delayed for long periods of time until peritonitis develops (Fossum & Descheneaux, 1991). Free intraperitoneal air is usually noted on abdominal radiographs. Retroperitoneal duodenal perforations are much more difficult to detect. Signs and symptoms may be subtle until retroperitoneal abscesses form.

Stomach Injuries. Rupture of the stomach has been described as resulting from child abuse (Case & Nanduri, 1983). Most of the lesions occur on the anterior surface. Gastric dilatation or eating a heavy meal before the injury may be a factor in precipitating gastric rupture with blunt injury. Gastric rupture leads to severe peritonitis as gastric contents leak into the abdominal cavity. Radiographic findings are similar to those found in intestinal perforations.

Liver Injuries. In one series, liver injury occurred in 47% of children with abdominal trauma from child abuse (Ledbetter et al., 1988). Liver trauma in children can be very difficult to diagnose (Suson et al., 1975). When children present with diffuse abdominal complaints and an *absence* of a history of trauma, the diagnosis may be missed, leading to disastrous consequence. Thus, the absence of a reliable history in cases of inflicted injury can complicate the diagnosis and treatment of liver injury.

Coant, Kornberg, Brody, and Edwards-Holmes (1992) studied serum transaminase enzyme levels (measure of liver function) in physically abused children who showed no signs of abdominal injury. They found a surprising 8% (4 of 49) of those children had elevated liver enzymes. Three of the four had occult liver lacerations. The authors concluded that liver trauma is more common than recognized in abused children and recommended liver function studies be done whenever concerns of acute abuse were presented. A more recent study of children with abdominal injuries (Isaacman et al., 1993), not necessarily related to abuse, found physical examination and urinalysis without blood tests to be adequate in the diagnosis of abdominal trauma. However, Coant et al.'s prospective study looked specifically at the problem of diagnosing injuries in abuse cases. The second study looked at an older age group, many of whom could report discomfort accurately. The results of the second study do not particularly address or refute the first study's conclusions.

Pancreatic Injuries. A spectrum of pancreatic injury has been described in cases of abusive trauma. Ledbetter et al. (1988) found pancreatic trauma in 12% of abused children with abdominal injuries. Pancreatitis (diffuse inflammation of the pancreas) can occur as a result of blunt trauma. As many as one third of cases of pancreatitis in children have been caused by abuse (Ziegler, Long, Philippart, & Klein, 1988).

One unusual complication of pancreatitis is the development of diffuse, osteolytic lesions throughout the skeleton, caused by the release of pancreatic enzymes into the blood stream (Cohen, Haller, & Friedman, 1981; Slovis, Berdon, Haller, Baker, & Rosen, 1975). The bony changes can be difficult to differentiate from those caused by skeletal trauma in abuse cases. Pancreatitis, abuse (or both), osteomyelitis, and malignancies can all cause similar radiographic patterns.

Pancreatic pseudocysts can result from pancreatitis caused by child abuse trauma (Kim & Jenkins, 1967). When the pancreas is disrupted, digestive enzymes can injure the pancreatic tissue itself, resulting in cystic structures that cause pain and bowel obstruction. Of pancreatic pseudocysts in children, 60% are attributable to trauma (Cooney & Grosfeld, 1975). This is probably a conservative estimate, considering that abusive trauma often goes unreported in the patient's history.

The pancreas can also be fractured or transected with child abuse trauma (Jenny & Hay, 1994; Tolia, Patel, & Amundson, 1990). Pancreatic inflammation and injury can be visualized with either ultrasonography or computerized tomography (Kaufman & Babcock, 1984). Measurement of serum levels of pancreatic enzymes is an important screening tool for the diagnosis of pancreatic injury.

Kidney and Bladder Trauma. Injuries to the urinary tract are not commonly reported in child abuse cases (Haller, Bass, & Sclafani, 1985; Ledbetter et al., 1988; Sirotnak, in press). When they do occur, they can be life threatening. The child's bladder is considered to be more vulnerable when blunt abdominal trauma occurs because of its higher position in the abdomen than is found in adults.

Other Injuries. Medullary hemorrhage of the adrenal glands has been reported to result from child abuse (Nimkin et al., 1994), as well as injuries to the large intestine. Although not frequently reported in the literature, I have cared for two abused children who exsanguinated from rupture of the aorta and vena cava respectively.

Imaging of Suspected Abuse-Related Trauma. For chest and abdominal trauma, CT is the most helpful modality. Ultrasound can be helpful in diagnosing occult duodenal, pancreatic, and kidney injuries. Occasionally, an upper gastrointestinal tract series may be required to diagnose duodenal hematomas (American Academy of Pediatrics, 1991).

STUDY QUESTIONS

1. How does abdominal trauma occur in cases of child abuse? What mortality rate does it carry?

2. Which of the solid organs is most likely to be injured in abusive trauma? What other organs might be injured?

3. Describe the presentation and tests needed for diagnosis of intra-abdominal trauma resulting from child abuse.

References

American Academy of Pediatrics, Section on Radiology. (1991). Diagnostic imaging of child abuse. *Pediatrics, 87,* 262-264.

Case, M. E. S., & Nanduri, R. (1983). Laceration of the stomach by blunt trauma in a child: A case of child abuse. *Journal of Forensic Sciences, 28,* 496-501.

Coant, P. N., Kornberg. A. E., Brody. A. S., & Edward-Holmes, K. (1992). Markers for occult liver injury in cases of physical abuse in children. *Pediatrics, 89,* 274-278.

Cobb, L. M., Vinocur, C. D., Wagner, C. W., & Weintraub, W. H. (1986). Intestinal perforation due to blunt trauma in children in an era of nonoperative treatment. *Journal of Trauma, 26,* 461-463.

Cohen, H., Haller, J. O., & Friedman, A. P. (1981). Pancreatitis, child abuse, and skeletal lesions. *Pediatric Radiology, 10,* 175-177.

Cooney, D. R., & Grosfeld, J. L. (1975). Operative management of pancreatic pseudo-cysts in infants and children: A review of 75 cases. *Annals of Surgery, 182,* 590-596.

Cooper, A. (1992). Thoracoabdominal trauma. In S. Ludwig & A. E. Kornberg (Eds.), *Child abuse: A medical reference* (pp. 131-149). New York: Churchill Living-stone.

Cooper, A., Floyd, T., Barlow, B., Niemirska, M., Ludwig, S., Seidl, T., O'Neill, J., Templeton, J., Ziegler, M., Ross, A., Gandhi, R., & Catherman, R. (1988). Major blunt abdominal trauma due to child abuse. *Journal of Trauma, 28,* 1483-1486.

Fossum, R. M., & Descheneaux, K. A. (1991). Blunt trauma of the abdomen in children. *Journal of Forensic Sciences, 36,* 47-50.

Haller, J. O., Bass, I. S., & Sclafani, S. J. (1985). Imaging evaluation of traumatic hematuria in children. *Urologic Radiology, 7,* 211-218.

Hermanz-Schulman, M., & Genieser, N. B. (1989). Sonographic diagnosis of intramural duodenal hematoma. *Journal of Ultrasound in Medicine, 8,* 273-276.

Isaacman, D. J., Scarfone, R. J., Kost, S. I., Gochman, R. F., Davis, H. W., Bernardo, L. M., & Nakayama, D. K. (1993). Utility of routine laboratory testing for detecting intra-abdominal injury in the pediatric trauma patient. *Pediatrics, 92,* 691-694.

Jenny, C., & Hay, T. C. (1994). *The visual diagnosis of child physical abuse.* Elk Grove Village, IL: American Academy of Pediatrics.

Jewett, T. C., Caldarola, V., Karp, M. P., Allen, J. E., & Cooney, D. R. (1988). Intramural hematoma of the duodenum. *Archives of Surgery, 123,* 54-58.

Kaufman, R. A., & Babcock, D. S. (1984). An approach to imaging the upper abdomen in the injured child. *Seminars in Roentgenology, 19,* 308-320.

Kim T., & Jenkins, M. E. (1967). Pseudocyst of the pancreas as a manifestation of the battered-child syndrome. Report of a case. *Medical Annals of District of Columbia, 36,* 664-666.

Kirks, D. R. (1983). Radiological evaluation of visceral injuries in the battered child syndrome. *Pediatric Annals, 12,* 888-893.

Kleinman, P. K. (1987). *Diagnostic imaging of child abuse* (pp. 116-133). Baltimore: Williams & Wilkins.

Kleinman, P. K., Raptopoulos, V. D., & Brill, P. W. (1981). Occult nonskeletal trauma in the battered-child syndrome. *Radiology, 141,* 393-396.

Ledbetter, D. J., Hatch, E. I., Feldman, K. W., Fligner, C. L., & Tapper, D. (1988). Diagnostic and surgical implications of child abuse. *Archives of Surgery, 123,* 1101-1105.

Nimkin, K., Teeger, S., Wallach, M. T., DuVally, J. C., Spevak, M. R., & Kleinman, P. K. (1994). Adrenal hemorrhage in abused children: Imaging and postmortem findings. *American Journal of Roentgenology, 162,* 661-663.

Sirotnak, A. P. (In press). Intraperitoneal bladder rupture: An uncommon manifestation of child abuse. *Clinical Pediatrics (Philadelphia).*

Slovis, T. L., Berdon, W. E., Haller, J. O., Baker, D. H., & Rosen, L. (1975). Pancreatitis and the battered child syndrome: Report of 2 cases with skeletal involvement. *American Journal of Roentgenology, 125,* 456-461.

Suson, E. M., Klotz, D. Jr., & Kottmeier, P. K. (1975). Liver trauma in children. *Journal of Pediatric Surgery, 10,* 411-417.

Tolia, V., Patel, A. S., & Amundson, G. M. (1990). Pancreatic fracture secondary to child abuse: The role of computed tomography in its diagnosis. *Clinical Pediatrics (Philadelphia), 11,* 667-668.

Ziegler, D. W., Long, J. A., Philippart, A. I., & Klein, M. D. (1988). Pancreatitis in childhood: Experience with 49 patients. *Annals of Surgery, 207,* 257-261.

Burns

Basic References

Erdmann, T. C., Feldman, K. W., Rivara, F. P., Heimbach, D. M., &
Wall, H. A. (1991). Tap water burn prevention: The effect of legislation. *Pediatrics, 88,* 572-577.

This article outlines the seriousness of tap water burns to children and
reports on a model prevention program.

Hammond, J., Perez-Stable, A., & Ward, C. G. (1991). Predictive value
of historical and physical characteristics for the diagnosis of child
abuse. *Southern Medical Journal, 84,* 166-168.

The clinical features distinguishing burn abuse from nonintentional burns
are reviewed, including a comprehensive prospective study of these factors.

Heimbach, D. M., Engrav, L. H., & Marvin, J. (1981). Minor burns: Guidelines for successful outpatient management. *Postgraduate Medicine, 69,* 22-26, 28-32.

A simple yet complete review of the assessment of burns, including descriptions of burn depth, causes of burns, and risk factors for bad outcomes.

Purdue, G. F., Hunt, J. L., & Prescott, P. R. (1988). Child abuse by burning: An index of suspicion. *Journal of Trauma, 28,* 221-224.

This study describes 71 children who were abused by burning. The authors review the clinical presentation and patterns of injury.

Weimer, C. L., Goldfarb, W., & Slater, H. (1988). Multidisciplinary approach to working with burn victims of child abuse. *Journal of Burn Care and Rehabilitation, 9,* 79-82.

The authors studied the emotional and social problems encountered when working with victims of burn abuse and their families.

Yeoh, C., Nixon, J. W., Dickson, W., Kemp, A., & Sibert, J. R. (1994). Patterns of scald injuries. *Archives of Diseases in Childhood, 71,* 156-158.

A critical study of scald injuries, the most common form of abusive burns.

Discussion

Burns are a common form of child abuse. The severity of a burn is measured by the depth of the burn and the percentage of the body surface area involved. The most frequently used categorization of burn depth relates to the layer of the skin affected (Heimbach, Engrav, & Marvin, 1981).

Epidermal burns (first degree) affect the epidermal layer of skin, causing redness but not blistering. They heal without scarring or treatment.

Partial thickness burns (second degree) involve the dermal layer of the skin, as well as the epidermal layer. However, some of the skin structures are maintained in the deep dermal layer, leaving hair follicles and sweat glands intact. These structures provide a source of new skin cells to cover the wound.

Superficial partial thickness burns heal without scarring, are very painful, and generally heal in less than 3 weeks.

Deep partial thickness burns also blister but are less painful because of the more extensive destruction of nerve fibers. There are fewer skin structures intact to regenerate new epithelium. Deep partial thickness burns usually are scarring and can be deforming. It is often difficult to discern superficial from deep partial thickness burns early in the course of therapy.

Full thickness burns (third degree) are painless and depressed. The dermis is completely destroyed, and skin regeneration occurs from the edges of the wound by contraction if not grafted. Full thickness burns cause scarring and loss of function.

PATTERNS OF BURNS
ASSOCIATED WITH CHILD ABUSE

Tap Water Immersion Burns. Child abuse burns are most commonly caused by immersion in hot tap water (Montry & Barcia, 1985; Purdue, Hunt, & Prescott, 1988). Inflicted tap water burns are most commonly found on the hands, feet, genitals, buttocks, and perineum (Hobbs, 1986). They are more likely to be bilateral and to have a clear "tide mark" at the edge of the burn and no splash marks, compared to accidental tap water burns, which usually have irregular edges and asymmetrical patterns (Yeoh, Nixon, Dickson, Kemp, & Sibert, 1994). Sparing of the flexor creases and of the body parts pressed against the bottom of a tub or sink can help determine the child's position while being burned (Lenoski & Hunter, 1977).

The depth of the burn depends on the temperature of the water and the length of time the child's body is submerged. When water is 125° Fahrenheit, adults will experience a partial thickness burn after 70 seconds of exposure. At 147° F, only 1 second of exposure is required to cause a full thickness burn (Moritz & Henriques, 1947). Most home water heaters are set to around 140° F. This would allow only 3 seconds of exposure to hot water before serious injury could occur. A successful tap water burn prevention program occurred in Washington State (Erdmann, Feldman, Rivara, Heimbach, & Wall, 1991). A state law was passed requiring that new home water heaters and water heaters in rental units be set at a lower temperature (120° F). This resulted in a significant decrease in the frequency, morbidity, and mortality of tap water burns. Although the rate of abuse-related burns did not decrease, such burns as a percentage of total burns increased from 31% to 50%. That is, the number of accidental burns declined.

Hot Liquid Splash Burns. These burns cause a characteristic appearance. The burn is worse at the initial point of contact, then decreases in severity as the liquid runs down the body. Many of these burns in children are accidental, caused by a child pulling down a container of hot liquid from a higher surface. Children in walkers are especially at risk of splashing hot liquids on themselves (Johnson, Ericson, & Caniano, 1990). Liquid grease burns are particularly damaging, because of the ability of the liquid to hold heat and stick to the skin.

Pattern (Contact) Burns. When hot objects are held onto a child's skin, the mark left will reflect the size and shape of the object. Cigarettes, electric irons, hair dryers (Prescott, 1990), heater grids, and cigarette lighters are examples of objects used to burn children (Raimer, Raimer, & Hebeler, 1981). As with other types of burns, the depth of the burn depends on the temperature of the object and the length of time the object is in contact with the skin. It is often difficult to distinguish nonintentional from inflicted pattern burns. Burns with clear margins, symmetrical burns, or multiple burns are more likely to be inflicted.

Flame Burns. Children can be burned purposefully by dousing them with flammable fluid or holding them over an open flame. I cared for one child who had both hands held over the gas flame on a kitchen stove. Smoke inhalation can complicate the course and treatment of flame burns. Burns sustained in a closed space, facial burns, pharyngeal debris, stridor, and respiratory distress should all alert the clinician to the possibility of significant smoke inhalation (Heimbach et al., 1981).

Heat Stroke. Heat stroke is another potentially catastrophic thermal injury among children. The characteristic signs of heat stroke are hyperpyrexia (rectal temperature greater than 106° F), delirium, coma, and anhidrosis (inability to sweat). In adults, the mortality rate after heat stroke is over 80% (Knochel, 1974). In children, the most common cause of heat stroke is being left in a parked car. Infants and small children are more susceptible to heat stroke than adults because of their larger surface area to weight ratio, causing excessive fluid losses, and their immature thermoregulatory control (Wadlington & Tucker, 1976). In addition, they are less likely to be able to move to a cool, safe place in times of heat stress.

Heat stroke leads to myocardial damage and circulatory collapse, liver and kidney failure, and cerebral edema and bleeding (Knochel, 1974). Although caused more often by neglect than by abuse, the prognosis for children experiencing heat stroke is usually grim.

TABLE 3.1 Factors Associated With Abusive Burns

Historical factors
  Burn attributed to sibling
  Child brought to the emergency room by a nonrelated adult
  Inappropriate parental affect
  Treatment delay
  Different historical accounts
  History of earlier accident
  Inappropriate affect of the child or an abnormal response to pain

Physical factors
  Injury inconsistent with history of the accident
  Injury inconsistent with child's chronological or developmental age
  "Mirror image" injuries
  Burns localized to the perineum, genitalia, or buttocks
  Injury appears older than the stated age
  Unrelated injuries, old or new

SOURCE: Hammond, Perez-Stable, and Ward (1991).

DIAGNOSING BURN ABUSE

Hammond, Perez-Stable, and Ward (1991) identified 7 historical factors and 6 physical factors associated with abuse by burning (see Table 3.1). The two most predictive factors were an injury inconsistent with the history given and a delay in seeking care. Of abusively burned children, 60% had two or more of the factors present.

PSYCHOLOGICAL FACTORS IN BURN ABUSE

Children with abusive burn injuries have been found to have a higher rate of depression than children with accidental burns (Campbell & LaClave, 1987). One study of abusively burned children showed 81% had receptive or expressive language deficits and 78% had decreased attention spans (Hammond, Nebel-Gold, & Brooks, 1989). Commonly, they were also noted to have inappropriate affect, irritability, withdrawn behavior, and tactile defensiveness.

Weimer, Goldfarb, and Slater (1988) studied the social problems found in abusive burn patients. They noted that 71% of the children were minorities with single mothers on public assistance. Many were born to adolescent parents, had a history of postnatal illness or prematurity, were physically or mentally handicapped, or had inadequate well-child care and immunizations.

These manifold social and emotional problems point out the importance of involving social work and mental health services in the care of these children. The above factors affect nursing care issues, including compliance, nutrition, and pain control.

STUDY QUESTIONS

1. How common are burns as a form of child abuse?

2. What types and patterns of burns are more likely to be associated with child abuse?

3. List the 13 characteristics of burn cases that increase the likelihood that the burn is a result of abuse.

References

Campbell, J. L., & LaClave, L. J. (1987). Clinical depression in pediatric burn patients. *Burns, 13,* 213-217.

Erdmann, T. C., Feldman, K. W., Rivara, F. P., Heimbach, D. M., & Wall, H. A. (1991). Tap water burn prevention: The effect of legislation. *Pediatrics, 88,* 572-577.

Hammond, J., Nebel-Gould, A., & Brooks, J. (1989). The value of speech-language assessment in the diagnosis of child abuse. *Journal of Trauma, 29,* 1258-1260.

Hammond, J., Perez-Stable, A., & Ward, C. G. (1991). Predictive value of historical and physical characteristics for the diagnosis of child abuse. *Southern Medical Journal, 84,* 166-168.

Heimbach, D. M., Engrav, L. H., & Marvin, J. (1981). Minor burns: Guidelines for successful outpatient management. *Postgraduate Medicine, 69,* 28-32.

Hobbs, C. J. (1986). When are burns not accidental. *Archives of Diseases in Childhood, 61,* 357-361.

Johnson, C. F., Ericson, A. K., & Caniano, D. (1990). Walker-related burns in infants and toddlers. *Pediatric Emergency Care, 6,* 58-61.

Knochel, J. P. (1974). Environmental heat illness: An eclectic review. *Archives of Internal Medicine, 133,* 841-864.

Lenoski, E. F., & Hunter, K. A. (1977). Specific patterns of inflicted burn injuries. *Journal of Trauma, 17,* 842-846.

Montry, J. S., & Barcia, P. J. (1985). Nonaccidental burns in child abuse. *Southern Medical Journal, 78,* 1324-1326.

Moritz, A. R., & Henriques, F. C. Jr. (1947). Studies of thermal energy, II: The relative importance of time and surface temperature in the causation of cutaneous burns. *American Journal of Pathology, 23,* 695-720.

Prescott, P. R. (1990). Hair dryer burns in children. *Pediatrics, 86,* 692-697.

Purdue, G. F., Hunt, H., & Prescott, P. R. (1988). Child abuse by burning: An index of suspicion. *Journal of Trauma, 28,* 221-224.

Raimer, B. G., Raimer, S. S., & Hebeler, J. R. (1981). Cutaneous signs of child abuse. *American Academy of Dermatology Journal, 5,* 203-214.

Wadlington, W. B., & Tucker, A. L. (1976). Heat stroke in infancy. *American Journal of Diseases in Children, 130,* 1250-1251.

Weimer, C. L., Goldfarb, W., & Slater, H. (1988). Multidisciplinary approach to working with burn victims of child abuse. *Journal of Burn Care and Rehabilitation, 9,* 79-82.

Yeoh, C., Nixon, J. W., Dickson, W., Kemp, A., & Sibert, J. R. (1994). Patterns of scald injuries. *Archives of Diseases in Childhood, 71,* 156-158.

Chest Injuries

Basic References

Very little has been written about thoracic injuries associated with child abuse. Individual case descriptions and case-specific references are listed below.

Discussion

Chest injuries are rarely recognized as a consequence of child abuse, other than rib fractures from squeezing and shaking an infant's thorax. The compliance and flexibility of the chest of young children allow for absorption of forces from direct blows (Cooper, 1992). In a review of all chest injuries seen at a children's hospital over a 20-year period, five cases of thoracic trauma were noted to have been caused by abuse, which amount to 7% of the total cases (Meller, Little, & Shermeta, 1984). The following thoracic and mediastinal injuries have been reported due to child physical abuse:

Lung Injuries

    Pulmonary contusion (McEniery, Hanson, Grigor, & Horowitz, 1991)

    Chylothorax (Green, 1980)

    Extrapleural hematoma (Jenny & Hay, 1994)

    Pleural effusion (Jenny & Hay, 1994)

    Hemothorax (Sivit, Taylor, & Eichelberger, 1989)

    Lung herniation (Jenny & Hay, 1994)

    Hydrocarbon pneumonia from induced poisoning (Saulsbury, Chobanian, & Wilson, 1984)

    Pneumothorax (Kleinman, Raptopoulos, & Brill, 1981)

    Fatal pepper aspiration (Cohle et al., 1988)

Heart Injuries

    Cardiomyopathy from ipecac administration (Goebel, Gremse, & Artman, 1993)

    Cardiac muscle hemorrhage and thrombus, with damage to the conduction system (Marino & Langston, 1982)

    Intimal tear of the right atrium (Cumberland, Riddick, & McConnell, 1991)

    Ventricular aneurysm (Rees, Symons, Joseph, & Lincoln, 1975)

    Needle insertion into the heart (Swadia, Thakore, Patel, & Bhavani, 1981)

Mediastinal Injuries

    Esophageal foreign bodies (Nolte, 1993)

    Esophageal perforation with mediastinal abscess (Ablin & Reinhart, 1990)

    Hemomediastinum (Cooper et al., 1988)

STUDY QUESTION

1. What is the presentation of intrathoracic trauma resulting from child abuse?

References

Ablin, D. S., & Reinhart, M. A. (1990). Esophageal perforation with mediastinal abscess in child abuse. *Pediatric Radiology, 20,* 524-525.

Cohle, S. D., Trestrall, J. D. III, Graham, M. A., Oxley, D. W., Walp, B., & Jachimezyk, F. (1988). Fatal pepper aspiration. *American Journal of Diseases of Children, 142,* 633-636.

Cooper, A. (1992). Thoracoabdominal trauma. In S. Ludwig & A. E. Kornberg (Eds.), *Child abuse: A medical reference* (p. 132). New York: Churchill Livingstone.

Cooper, A., Floyd, T., Barlow, B., Niemirska, M., Ludwig, S., Seidl, T., O'Neill, J., Templeton, J., Ziegler, M., Ross, A., Gandhi, R., & Catherman, R. (1988). Major blunt abdominal trauma due to child abuse. *Journal of Trauma, 28,* 1483-1486.

Cumberland, G. D., Riddick, L., & McConnell, C. F. (1991). Intimal tears of the right atrium of the heart due to blunt force injuries to the abdomen: Its mechanism and implications. *American Journal of Forensic Medicine and Pathology, 12,* 102-104.

Goebel, J., Gremse, D. A., & Artman, M. (1993). Cardiomyopathy from ipecac administration in Munchausen syndrome by proxy. *Pediatrics, 92,* 601-603.

Green, H. G. (1980). Child abuse presenting as chylothorax. *Pediatrics, 66,* 620-621.

Jenny, C., & Hay, T. C. (1994). *The visual diagnosis of child physical abuse.* Elk Grove Village, IL: American Academy of Pediatrics.

Kleinman, P. K., Raptopoulos, V. D., & Brill, P. W. (1981). Occult nonskeletal trauma in the battered-child syndrome. *Radiology, 141,* 393-396.

Marino, T. A., & Langston, C. (1982). Cardiac trauma and the conduction system. *Archives of Pathology and Laboratory Medicine, 106,* 173-174.

McEniery, J., Hanson, R., Grigor, W., & Horowitz, A. (1991). Lung injury resulting from a nonaccidental crush injury to the chest. *Pediatric Emergency Care, 7,* 166-168.

Meller, J. L., Little, A. G., & Shermeta, D. W. (1984). Thoracic trauma in children. *Pediatrics, 74,* 813-819.

Nolte, K. B. (1993). Potential fatal mechanisms: Esophageal foreign bodies as child abuse. *American Journal of Forensic Medicine and Pathology, 14,* 323-326.

Rees, A., Symons, J., Joseph, M., & Lincoln, C. (1975). Ventricular septal defect in a battered child. *British Medical Journal, 1,* 20-21.

Saulsbury, F. T., Chobanian, M. C., & Wilson, W. G. (1984). Child abuse: Parental hydrocarbon administration. *Pediatrics, 73,* 719-721.

Sivit, C. J., Taylor, G. A., & Eichelberger, M. R. (1989). Visceral injury in battered children: A changing perspective. *Radiology, 173,* 659-661.

Swadia, N. D., Thakore, A. B., Patel, B. R., & Bhavani, S. S. (1981). Unusual form of child abuse presenting as an acute abdomen. *British Journal of Surgery, 68,* 668.

5

Injuries to the Face, Ears, Mouth, Throat, and Nose

Basic References

American Academy of Pediatrics, Committee on Early Childhood, Adoption, and Dependent Care. (1986). Oral and dental aspects of child abuse and neglect. *Pediatrics, 78,* 537-539.

The American Academy of Pediatrics issued this statement to emphasize the importance of recognizing oral injuries caused by child abuse.

Becker, D. B., Needleman, H. L., & Kotelchuck, M. (1978). Child abuse and dentistry: Orofacial trauma and its recognition by dentists. *American Dental Association Journal, 97,* 24-28.

Becker and colleagues reviewed a wide series of cases involving abused children with injuries to the mouth and face.

29

Grace, A., & Grace, M. A. (1987). **Child abuse within the ear, nose, and throat.** *Journal of Otolaryngology, 16,* 108-111.

This study presents case reports and provides a complete review of the spectrum of injuries from child abuse to the ears, nose, and throat.

Needleman, H. L. (1986). **Orofacial trauma in child abuse: Types, prevalence, management, and the dental profession's involvement.** *Pediatric Dentistry, 8*(S-1), 71-79.

This article provides an excellent review of the literature regarding orofacial trauma in abused children.

Discussion

Orofacial trauma is commonly encountered in physically abused children. A retrospective review of a series of cases has shown that from 49% to 68% of physical abuse cases involve trauma to the face, mouth, or both (Becker, Needleman, & Kotelchuck, 1978; Elging, Bower, & Cotton, 1992). The face is more likely to be traumatized because of its psychological significance when a child confronts a parent or cries out against the physical and emotional pain of abuse (Symons, Rowe, & Romaniuk, 1987). In addition, the mouth is a common site of injury when parents and children fight over the intake of food.

Becker et al. (1978) surveyed orofacial trauma in 260 cases of abused children admitted to a children's hospital. As shown in Table 5.1, they found the following distribution of injuries.

Facial Contusions. In this study, facial contusions were seen twice as often as the next most frequent injury, contusions to the body and internal organs. In reviewing 29 cases of fatal child abuse, Cameron, Johnson, and Camps (1966) found soft tissue injury to the forehead in 52% of the cases, to the cheeks in 48%, to the upper lip in 45%, and to the lower jaw in 48%. Specific types of orofacial injuries are discussed next.

Injuries to the Lips. Forcing objects into a child's mouth or directly hitting the mouth can cause tears of the frenula of the lips or tearing of the lips from the alveolar margins of the gums (Cameron, Johnson, & Camps, 1966).

TABLE 5.1 Distribution of Orofacial Trauma in Children Admitted for
Child Abuse

Location	Injury Type	Number	Percentage
Face		145	91
	Fractures	3	2
	Abrasions/Lacerations	40	25
	Contusions/Bruises	96	60
	Burns	4	3
	Bites	2	1
Intraoral		14	9
	Abrasions/Lacerations	4	3
	Contusions/Bruises	6	3
	Dental trauma	4	3

SOURCE: Becker, Needleman, and Kotelchuck, (1978).

Although frenula tears are not uncommon in children who accidentally fall
while learning to walk (usually children ages 6 months to 1.5 years), these
injuries in not yet ambulatory children or in older, motorically steady children
are highly suspicious as cases of abuse (Needleman, 1986).

Soft tissue contusions, lacerations, or abrasions can be caused by direct
blows or by a child being pushed into a hard object. Holding a hand over a
child's mouth to stifle a cry or attempt to suffocate the child can leave
tooth-shaped lesions on the inner lip. The corners of the mouth can be
abraded when a gag is tied around the child's head. Thermal and chemical
burns to the face and oropharynx can occur when a child is forced to drink
hot or caustic liquids (Reece, 1990).

Injuries to the Teeth. Injuries to the teeth include avulsion or fracture, as
well as abnormal tooth development or eruption based on previous trauma.
Malocclusion can also result from healing trauma (Symons et al., 1987).

Injuries to the Tongue. The tongue can be bitten during an assault.
Purposeful laceration of the tongue has been reported as an abusive injury
(Jenny & Hay, 1994). The frenulum of the tongue can be ruptured when
objects are forced into the mouth (Jenny & Hay, 1994).

Facial Bone Fractures. Facial fractures are uncommon in children. However, a physical assault can result in facial fractures. In one series, the most

common site of fracture was the nose (45%), followed by the mandible (32%) and the zygoma and orbit (20.5%) (Kaban, Mulliken, & Murray, 1977). Siegel, Wetmore, Potsic, Handler, and Tom (1991) found that 14% of mandibular fractures in children were caused by child abuse. Abusive facial fractures in children can lead to abnormal facial growth and facial malformations (Precious, Delaire, & Hoffman, 1988).

Injuries to the Palate, Pharynx, Hypopharynx, and Larynx. Several cases have been reported of children sustaining lacerations, abrasions or both to the mouth, uvula, and throat from forcefully inserted foreign bodies (Grace & Grace, 1987; Manning, Casselbrant, & Lammers, 1990). A foreign body lodged in the hypopharynx can cause severe failure-to-thrive in an infant (Buckler & Stool, 1967). Hypopharyngeal lacerations can cause interstitial emphysema of the head and neck, as well as retropharyngeal abscesses and mediastinitis (Kleinman, Spevak, & Hansen, 1992; McDowell & Fielding, 1984). Abusive pharyngeal trauma has been reported to result in pharyngeal obstruction and atrophy (Morris & Reay, 1971). Lacerations of the palate can result from forced fellatio (Casamassimo, 1986). Vocal cord paralysis has been reported to be caused by both strangulation and head injury (Myer & Fitton, 1988).

Injuries to the Nose. In addition to nasal fractures, loss of the nasal septum and columella have been reported to result from repeated abusive blunt trauma to the nose and from abusive, repetitive scouring of the nose with a bobby pin (Orton, 1975; Pincus & Bukachevsky, 1990).

Injuries to the Ear. Direct and tangential blows to the ear can cause bruising and petechiae to the external ear, possibly from the apex of the helix folding onto itself and being crimped against the head (Feldman, 1992; Hanigan, Peterson, & Njus, 1987). With severe, repetitive injury, deformation and scarring of the external ear can occur, including "cauliflower ear" resulting from organized hematomas retracting the ear structure (Pincus & Bukachevsky, 1990; Willner, Ledereich, & deVries, 1992). The attachment of the earlobe can be severed from the side of the head (Willner et al., 1992).

Internal injuries to the tympanic membrane can be caused by foreign bodies and by "cupping" or concussive injuries (Manning et al., 1990; Obiako, 1987). With inflicted eardrum lacerations, the external auditory canal may be lacerated as well (Grace, Kalinkiewicz, & Drake-Lee, 1984). Hemotympanum has been known to occur after external blows to the ear. Occasionally, blows to the side of the head can be severe enough to disrupt the ossicles in the internal ear (Grace & Grace, 1987).

STUDY QUESTIONS

1. How common is orofacial trauma in physically abused children?
2. What are the common patterns of injury inflicted to the face, ears, mouth, nose, and throat of an abused child?

References

Becker, D. B., Needleman, H. L., & Kotelchuck, M. (1978). Child abuse and dentistry: Orofacial trauma and its recognition by dentists. *American Dental Association Journal, 97*, 24-28.

Buckler, J. M., & Stool, S. E. (1967). Failure to thrive: An exogenous cause. *American Journal of Diseases of Children, 114*, 652-653.

Cameron, J. M., Johnson, H. R., & Camps, F. E. (1966). The battered child syndrome. *Medical Science Law, 6*, 2-21.

Casamassimo, P. S. (1986). Child sexual abuse and the pediatric dentist. *Pediatric Dentistry, 8*(S-1), 102-106.

Elging, J. P., Bower, C. M., & Cotton, R. T. (1992). Physical abuse of children. A retrospective review and an otolaryngology perspective. *Archives of Otolaryngology, Head & Neck Surgery, 118*, 584-590.

Feldman, K. W. (1992). Patterned abusive bruises of the buttocks and the pinnae. *Pediatrics, 90*, 633-636.

Grace, A., & Grace, M. A. (1987). Child abuse within the ear, nose, and throat. *Journal of Otolaryngology, 16*, 108-111.

Grace, A., Kalinkiewicz, M., & Drake-Lee, A. B. (1984). Covert manifestations of child abuse. *British Medical Journal (Clinical Research), 289*, 1041-1042.

Hanigan, W. C., Peterson, R. A., & Njus, G. (1987). Tin ear syndrome: Rotational acceleration in pediatric head injuries. *Pediatrics, 80*, 618-622.

Jenny, C., & Hay, T. C. (1994). *The visual diagnosis of child physical abuse*. Elk Grove Village, IL: American Academy of Pediatrics.

Kaban, L. B., Mulliken, J. B., & Murray, J. E. (1977). Facial fractures in children. *Plastic Reconstructive Surgery, 59*, 15-20.

Kleinman, P. K., Spevak, M. R., & Hansen, M. (1992). Mediastinal pseudocyst caused by pharyngeal perforation during child abuse. *American Journal of Roentgenology, 158*, 1111-1113.

Manning, S. C., Casselbrant, M., & Lammers, D. (1990). Otolaryngologic manifestations of child abuse. *International Journal of Pediatric Otorhinolaryngology, 20*, 7-16.

McDowell, H. P., & Fielding, D. W. (1984). Traumatic perforation of the hypopharynx: An unusual form of abuse. *Archives of Diseases in Childhood, 59,* 888-889.

Morris, T. M., & Reay, H. A. (1971). A battered baby with pharyngeal atresia. *Journal of Laryngology and Otology, 85,* 729-731.

Myer, C. M., III, Fitton, C. M. (1988). Vocal cord paralysis following child abuse. *International Journal of Pediatric Otorhinolaryngology, 15,* 217-220.

Needleman, H. L. (1986). Orofacial trauma in child abuse: Types, prevalence, management, and the dental profession's involvement. *Pediatric Dentistry, 8*(S-1), 71-79.

Obiako, M. N. (1987). Eardrum perforation as evidence of child abuse. *Child Abuse & Neglect, 11,* 149-151.

Orton, C. I. (1975). Loss of columella and septum from an unusual form of child abuse: Case report. *Plastic Reconstructive Surgery, 56,* 345-346.

Pincus, R. L., & Bukachevsky, R. P. (1990). Medially based horizontal nasolabial flaps for reconstruction of columellar defects. *Archives of Otolaryngology, Head and Neck Surgery, 116,* 973-974.

Precious, D. S., Delaire, J., & Hoffman, C. D. (1988). The effects of nasomaxillary injury on future facial growth. *Oral Surgery, Oral Medicine, and Oral Pathology, 66,* 525-530.

Reece, R. M. (1990). Unusual manifestations of child abuse. *Pediatric Clinics of North America, 37,* 905-922.

Siegel, M. B., Wetmore, R. F., Potsic, W. P., Handler, S. D., & Tom, L. W. (1991). Mandibular fractures in the pediatric patient. *Archives of Otolaryngology, Head & Neck Surgery, 117,* 533-536.

Symons, A. L., Rowe, P. V., & Romaniuk, K. (1987). Dental aspects of child abuse: Review and case reports. *Australian Dental Journal, 32,* 42-47.

Willner, A., Ledereich, P. S., & deVries, E. J. (1992). Auricular injury as a presentation of child abuse. *Archives of Otolaryngology, Head and Neck Surgery, 118,* 634-637.

Fractures

Basic References

American Academy of Pediatrics, Section on Radiology. (1991). Diagnostic imaging of child abuse. *Pediatrics, 87, 262-264.*

The Academy of Pediatrics has issued a policy statement on radiological procedures in the evaluation of abuse. The concepts in the article are essential to understanding the proper use of diagnostic imaging in suspected abuse.

Chapman, S. (1990). Radiological aspects of nonaccidental injury. *Journal of the Royal Society of Medicine, 83, 67-71.*

This article contains a well-thought-out discussion of illnesses that cause fractures that may simulate abusive injuries.

Chapman, S. (1992). The radiological dating of injuries. *Archives of Diseases in Childhood, 67, 1063-1065.*

This article reviews the important points to consider when dating injuries.

Kleinman, P. K. (1987). *Diagnostic imaging of child abuse.* **Baltimore: Williams & Wilkins.**

This book is the definitive text on the radiology of abuse. It is currently out of print but is available in most medical libraries.

Tufts, E., Blank, E., & Dickerson, D. (1982). Periosteal thickening as a manifestation of trauma in infancy. *Child Abuse & Neglect,* **6,** **359-364.**

This classic article explains the importance of identifying and recognizing periosteal lesions as a sign of abuse.

Discussion

Any fracture can be caused by abuse or by nonintentional trauma. However, certain fractures occur very frequently in abuse cases and are rarely seen as a result of accidents. It is important to understand the pathogenesis and mechanism of injury in those fractures virtually pathognomonic of abuse.

PATHOLOGICAL CATEGORIZATION OF FRACTURES

Periosteal Elevation

The periosteum is a thick, fibrous membrane covering the outer surface of the bone. When children are handled roughly (e.g., pulling or twisting the extremities or severe shaking), the periosteum can pull away from the bone, causing bleeding between the bone and the periosteum. Initially, no changes will be seen on radiographs other than soft-tissue swelling. Kleinman states that new bone begins to form under the periosteum in 5 to 14 days, at which time the lesions can be visualized on X rays (Kleinman, 1987). Although periosteal elevation is not specific for abuse, it is not commonly seen in nonabused children (Tufts, Blank, & Dickerson, 1982).

Fractures of the Diaphysis (Shaft) of the Long Bones

The pattern of diaphyseal fractures of the long bones generally reflects the type of force applied to the bone. Spiral fractures involve rotational forces, and transverse fractures imply translational forces, whereas compression fractures result from axial loading. All of these types of fractures can be caused by abuse or by accident. Previously, spiral fractures of the long bones were considered pathognomonic of abuse. However, these fractures can also occur in toddlers who fall when running or walking (Thomas, Rosenfield, Leventhal, & Markowitz, 1991). One well-documented case of an accidental spiral fracture of the humerus of an infant occurred when the child's sibling turned him over, catching his arm underneath him in the process. The parents were videotaping the children playing at the time (Hymel & Jenny, 1996).

Metaphyseal Fractures

On radiographs, fractures at the ends of the shafts of the long bones, where the shaft joins the growth plate, appear as "corner fractures" or "bucket handle-shaped fractures." They are caused by microfractures occurring in the immature metaphyseal bone at the zone of provisional calcification (Kleinman, Marks, & Blackbourne, 1986). These fractures usually occur in children less than 2 years old. Metaphyseal fractures are almost always associated with child abuse and are rarely seen in accidental injuries.

Other Types of Fractures

Besides metaphyseal fractures, Kleinman (1987) identifies nine other types of fractures that are highly or moderately specific for abuse:

Posterior Rib Fractures. Rib fractures in abused children are most often located near the costo-transverse process articulation (where the rib heads articulate with the spine). They are most likely caused by compression forces on the chest (grabbing and squeezing, often during shaking of the child) (Kleinman, Marks, Spevak, & Richmond, 1992). Lateral rib fractures can occur by the same mechanism.

Abusive rib fractures are difficult to identify in infants until callus begins to form at the fracture site (Kleinman, Marks, Adams, & Blackbourne, 1988). Repeat rib X rays in suspected abuse cases days or weeks after the injury may reveal previously missed fractures. Rib fractures can also be identified at autopsy that are not radiographically visible. Radioisotopic bone scans may be useful in detecting early rib fractures before callus develops (Smith, Gilday, Ash, & Green, 1980). Rib fractures have not been shown to be caused by cardiopulmonary resuscitation in infants (Feldman & Brewer, 1984; Spevak, Kleinman, Belanger, Primack, & Richmond, 1994).

Scapular Fractures. The acromion process is the most commonly fractured part of the scapula in infants, although fractures of the coracoid process or scapular body can also occur. In the absence of severe, direct blows to the shoulder, scapular fractures are not likely to be accidental. The mechanism of injury is thought to be forced traction or rotation of an infant's upper extremity.

Spinous Process Fractures. With violent shaking, avulsion of bony fragments from the posterior spinous processes can occur (Kleinman & Zito, 1970). The area where the interspinous ligament attaches to the bony prominences tears from the rapid spinal flexion and extension with shaking. These fractures can be subtle and very difficult to detect.

Sternal Fractures. Fractures of the sternum are rare and imply massive forces applied to the chest wall.

Multiple Fractures and Fractures of Different Ages. When more than one unexplained fracture is identified on a child, abuse is likely to be the cause. This is especially true if the fractures are of different ages. Although the differential diagnosis of pathological fractures is extensive, most of the organic diseases causing multiple fractures are rare. (See the following discussion of differential diagnosis of fractures.)

Epiphyseal Plate Injuries. Growth plate injuries have been reported as child abuse injuries, particularly of the humerus (Akbarnia, Silberstein, Rende, Graviss, & Luisiri, 1986; DeLee, Wilkins, Rogers, & Rockwood, 1980; Merten, Kirks, & Ruderman, 1981; Thompson & Gesler, 1984). These injuries can be very difficult to diagnose because of the lack of ossification of the ends of the long bones. Growth plate injuries can cause growth arrest of the extremities and subsequent deformities.

Vertebral Body Fractures and Subluxations. Compression fractures of the spine of infants can be caused by violent shaking (Kleinman & Marks, 1992). During shaking, the hyperflexion of the spine causes the fractures to occur. Other spinal abnormalities have been attributed to abuse, including fractures of the sacral spine from slamming a child down on a hard surface in a sitting position, vertebral dislocation, herniation of vertebral disks (Schwischuk, 1969), and subluxation of the spine. One child whom I cared for had a complete rupture of the anterior longitudinal ligament of the spine, suspected to have been caused by a kick in the back that hyperextended the spine.

TABLE 6.1 Differential Diagnosis of Fractures

Disease	Shaft Fracture	Abnormal Metaphysis	Osteopenia	Periosteal Reaction	Comments
Child abuse	+	+	−	+	
Accidental trauma	+	−	−	−	
Birth trauma	+	+/−	−	+/−	Clavicle, humerus, and femur are the most frequent fractures
Osteogenesis imperfecta	+	+/−	+	callus	Highly unlikely in the absence of osteopenia, Wormian bones, dentinogenesis imperfecta, and a relevant family history
Osteomyelitis	−	+	localized	+	May be multifocal
Rickets	+	+	+	+	Increased alkaline phosphatase
Scurvy	−	+	+	+	Not before age 6 months
Congenital syphilis	−	+	−	+	
Congenital insensitivity to pain	+	+	−	+	
Myelodysplasia	+	+	−	+	Spinal dysraphism
Prostaglandin E therapy	−	−	−	+	
Menke's disease	−	+	+	+	Males only. Abnormal hair, retardation, Wormian bones
Copper deficiency	+	+	+	+/−	Rare condition
Caffey's syndrome	+	−	−	++	Mandible usually involved
Leukemia	−	−	+	+	Bone changes extremely variable
Methotrexate therapy	−	+/−	++	−	Unlikely to occur with current regimens

SOURCES: Chapman (1990) and Brill and Winchester (1987).

Digital Fractures. Fractures of the small bones of the hands and feet can be caused by abusive crush or squeezing injuries (Jaffe & Lasser, 1977; Rao & Hyde, 1984). One case described small bone fractures from rapping of a child's knuckles (Kleinman, 1987).

Complex Skull Fractures. See the discussion in Chapter 7 of head injuries.

DIFFERENTIAL DIAGNOSIS OF FRACTURES

Chapman provides a thoughtful overview of the difference between abuse and nonabuse fractures. Table 6.1 is taken from his 1990 article in the *Journal of the Royal Society of Medicine* and from a similar table by Brill and Winchester in Kleinman's 1987 book, *Diagnostic Imaging of Child Abuse.*

IMAGING ISSUES

The American Academy of Pediatrics has issued guidelines for radiological imaging in suspected child abuse cases (American Academy of Pediatrics, 1991). These guidelines make several specific recommendations regarding radiographical skeletal surveys. Skeletal surveys should be obtained, using carefully selected techniques and imaging systems to maximize the likelihood that subtle fractures can be detected. Pediatric "body grams," whereby the child's body is X-rayed on a single film, are unacceptable. An adequate skeletal survey should include separate exposures of the anteroposterior view of the arms, forearms, hands, femurs, lower legs, and feet; lateral and frontal views of the axial skeleton; and anteroposterior and lateral views of the skull.

Skeletal surveys are mandatory in all cases of suspected physical abuse in children under 2 years of age. Beyond 5 years of age, the skeletal survey is seldom helpful. From 2 through 4 years of age, the decision of whether or not to obtain a skeletal survey can be individualized, depending on the clinical presentation.

Radionuclide bone scans can be helpful in diagnosing occult fractures (Sty & Starshak, 1983). It is quite sensitive in diagnosing rib fractures and long bone fractures. However, it is less useful in the diagnosis of metaphyseal fractures.

HEALING OF FRACTURES

The healing process of fractures of the long bones follows a well-defined histologic sequence, beginning with hemorrhage and soft tissue swelling, then tissue metaplasia, formation of soft callus, formation of hard callus, and finally, remodeling of the bone (Chapman, 1992). Although there is some variability in the rates of healing between individuals, broad guidelines exist on the timing of injury. Generally, infants and young children heal faster than adults (Connor & Cohen, 1987).

Metaphyseal fractures generally heal without forming callus. In these fractures, the periosteum is not generally disrupted, making them difficult to age radiologically. Histopathological studies on autopsy specimens of metaphyseal fractures in abused infants have shown specific microscopic bone changes associated with the healing fractures (metaphyseal extensions of hypertrophied chondrocytes). Although information on the rapidity of these changes after injury is not yet available, further research may allow more accurate timing of metaphyseal injuries (Osier, Marks, & Kleinman, 1993). Skull fractures are difficult to date, because callus does not form at the fracture line.

STUDY QUESTIONS

1. What are the common patterns of fractures found in child abuse?
2. What are the stages of healing seen in bone injuries?
3. What are the diseases that can cause pathological fractures resembling those found in abused children?

References

Akbarnia, B. A., Silberstein, M. J., Rende, R. J., Graviss, E. R., & Luisiri, A. (1986). Arthrography in the diagnosis of fractures of the distal end of the humerus in infants. *Journal of Bone and Joint Surgery (American Volume)*, 68, 699-602.

American Academy of Pediatrics, Section on Radiology. (1991). Diagnostic imaging of child abuse. *Pediatrics*, 87, 262-264.

Brill, P. W., & Winchester, P. (1987). Differential diagnosis of child abuse. In P. K. Kleinman (Ed.), *Diagnostic imaging of child abuse* (p. 222). Baltimore: Williams & Wilkins.

Chapman, S. (1990). Radiological aspects of non-accidental injury. *Journal of the Royal Society of Medicine*, 83, 67-71.

Chapman, S. (1992). The radiological dating of injuries. *Archives of Diseases in Childhood*, 67(9), 1063-1065.

Connor, J. F., & Cohen, J. (1987). Dating fractures. In P. K. Kleinman (Ed.), *Diagnostic imaging of child abuse* (pp. 103-113). Baltimore: Williams & Wilkins.

DeLee, J. C., Wilkins, K. E., Rogers, L. F., & Rockwood, C. A. (1980). Fracture-separation of the distal humeral epiphysis. *Journal of Bone and Joint Surgery (American Volume)*, 62, 46-51.

Feldman, K. W., & Brewer, D. K. (1984). Child abuse, cardiopulmonary resuscitation, and rib fractures. *Pediatrics*, 73, 339-342.

Jaffe, A. C., & Lasser, D. H. (1977). Multiple metatarsal fractures in child abuse. *Pediatrics*, 60, 642-643.

Kleinman, P. K. (1987). *Diagnostic imaging of child abuse* (pp. 5-10, 62). Baltimore: Williams & Wilkins.

Kleinman, P. K., & Marks, S. C. (1992). Vertebral body fractures in child abuse: Radiologic-histopathologic correlates. *Investigative Radiology, 27,* 715-722.

Kleinman, P. K., Marks, S. C., Adams, V. I., & Blackbourne, B. D. (1988). Factors affecting visualization of posterior rib fractures in abused infants. *American Journal of Roentgenology, 150,* 635-638.

Kleinman, P. K., Marks, S. C., & Blackbourne, B. (1986). The metaphyseal lesion in abused infants: A radiologic-histopathologic study. *American Journal of Roentgenology, 146,* 895-905.

Kleinman, P. K., Marks, S. C., Spevak, M. R., & Richmond, J. M. (1992). Fractures of the rib head in abused infants. *Radiology, 185,* 119-123.

Kleinman, P. K., & Zito, J. L. (1970). Avulsion of the spinous processes caused by infant abuse. *Radiology, 95,* 661-664.

Merten, D. F., Kirks, D. R., & Ruderman, R. J. (1981). Occult humeral epiphyseal fracture in battered infants. *Pediatric Radiology, 10,* 151-154.

Osier, L. K., Marks, S. C., & Kleinman, P. K. (1993). Metaphyseal extensions of hypertrophied chondrocytes in abused infants indicate healing fractures. *Journal of Pediatric Orthopedics, 13,* 249-254.

Rao, K. S., & Hyde, I. (1984). Digital lesions in non-accidental injuries in children. *British Journal of Radiology, 57,* 259-260.

Schwischuk, L. E. (1969). Spine and spinal cord trauma in the battered child syndrome. *Radiology, 92,* 733-738.

Smith, F. W., Gilday, D. L., Ash, J. M., & Green, M. D. (1980). Unsuspected costo-vertebral fractures demonstrated by bone scanning in the child abuse syndrome. *Pediatric Radiology, 10,* 103-106.

Spevak, M. R., Kleinman, P. K., Belanger, P. L., Primack, C., & Richmond, J. M. (1994). Cardiopulmonary resuscitation and rib fractures in infants. A postmortem radiologic-pathologic study. *Journal of the American Medical Association, 272,* 617-618.

Sty, J. R., & Starshak, R. J. (1983). The role of bone scintigraphy in the evaluation of the suspected abused child. *Radiology, 146,* 369-375.

Thomas, S. A., Rosenfield, N. S., Leventhal, J. M., & Markowitz, R. I. (1991). Long bone fractures in young children: Distinguishing accidental injuries from child abuse. *Pediatrics, 88,* 471-476.

Thompson, G. H., & Gesler, J. W. (1984). Proximal tibial epiphyseal fracture in an infant. *Journal of Pediatric Orthopedics, 4,* 114-117.

Tufts, E., Blank, E., & Dickerson, D. (1982). Periosteal thickening as a manifestation of trauma in infancy. *Child Abuse & Neglect, 6,* 359-364.

Head Injuries

The works cited here as "must reads" were selected to give a broad overview of the issues involved in understanding abusive head trauma. Several of the articles cited are classics in the field. Although they were published years ago, they are certainly not dated and provide a perspective that still guides our thinking.

Basic References

Alexander, R., Sato, Y., Smith, W., & Bennett, T. (1990). Incidence of impact trauma with cranial injuries ascribed to shaking. *American Journal of Diseases of Children, 144,* 724-726.

In regard to shaken baby syndrome, this article presents the opposite view of Duhaime et al. listed below.

American Academy of Pediatrics, Committee on Child Abuse and Neglect. (1993). Shaken baby syndrome: Inflicted cerebral trauma. *Pediatrics, 92,* 872-875.

The American Academy of Pediatrics has issued this "position paper" on shaken baby syndrome.

> **Brown, J. K., & Minns, R. A. (1993). Non-accidental head injury, with particular reference to whiplash shaking injury and medico-legal aspects.** *Developmental Medicine in Child Neurology, 35*, 849-869.

Brown and Minns provide a helpful review article on abusive head trauma. Of particular interest is their section on forensic issues and the estimation of the time head injuries occurred based on clinical and pathological factors.

> **Caffey, J. (1972). On the theory and practice of shaking infants.** *American Journal of Diseases of Children, 124*, 161-169.

This article by Caffey continues to guide our conceptualization of shaken baby syndrome.

> **Duhaime, A. C., Gennarelli, T. A., Thibault, L. E., Bruce, D. A., Margulies, S. S., & Wiser, R. (1987). The shaken baby syndrome: A clinical, pathological, and biomechanical study.** *Journal of Neurosurgery, 66*, 409-415.

This article presents evidence that impact is required to cause the degree of pathology seen in shaken baby syndrome.

> **Dykes, L. J. (1986). The whiplash shaken infant syndrome: What has been learned?** *Child Abuse & Neglect, 10*, 211-221.

This article provides a superb overview of research on shaken baby syndrome.

> **Hardman, J. M. (1979). The pathology of traumatic brain injuries.** *Advances in Neurology, 22*, 15-50.

This article reviews the pathological changes seen in brain trauma. Tables review the progression of changes after head injury and can be useful in interpreting autopsy data in child abuse cases.

> **Vowles, G. H., Scholtz, C. L., & Cameron, J. M. (1987). Diffuse axonal injury in early infancy.** *Journal of Clinical Pathology, 40*, 185-189.

When this article is read along with Hardman's review, the reader will have a broad understanding of the pathological changes that occur after abusive head trauma.

Discussion

Abusive head trauma is the most lethal form of child abuse. Not only do children with impact and shaking trauma to the head often die, many victims are left with permanent debilitating neurological diseases, such as cerebral palsy, seizure disorders, blindness, or deafness (Sarsfield, 1974). Many years of clinical experience culminated in the discovery of the mechanisms of shaking and battering of infants in the development of signs and symptoms of head trauma. In 1946, John Caffey wrote a stunningly insightful article reviewing six cases of infants with subdural hematomas and multiple fractures. He speculated how these children could have sustained such serious injury in the absence of a history of major trauma.

In 1972, Dr. Caffey reviewed the evidence that "whiplash shaking" of infants can cause subdural hematomas and severe brain injury. He cited several fatal cases of head injuries caused by a hired infant nurse who cared for children "of upper-middle-class, well-educated, well-to-do parents." The nurse admitted to killing three infants and maiming 12 others, "largely by shaking and jolting infantile brains and their blood vessels."

Parents often report picking up infants by the chest or shoulders and shaking them in anger or frustration. Some of them will admit to shaking the infant on multiple occasions. Many parents know that gentle up-and-down or rocking motion can help calm a baby. Violent shaking also quiets babies but probably does so by causing brain injury. The shaking episodes parents describe that lead to severe injuries are not similar to the kind of calm, repetitive movements used in the course of normal infant care. Even rough-housing or tossing an infant up into the air is unlikely to cause injuries. Violent, rough, repetitive, angry movements lead to subdural hematomas, retinal hemorrhages, and fractures.

VULNERABILITY OF INFANTS TO HEAD INJURY

Several factors make young infants more vulnerable to head injury by shaking (Dykes, 1986). First, the infant brain is softer than a mature brain. Neurons are not yet fully developed. Unmyelinated nerves are more plastic and vulnerable. Second, infants have more cerebrospinal fluid surrounding the brain, allowing for more movement of the brain within the skull with shaking. Third, infants have proportionately larger heads compared to their body weight than adults. This large head is poorly supported by weak neck muscles. When the infant is shaken, the head whips back and forth in an arc and the brain experiences rotational as well as translational forces. In addition, the small size and body weight of the infant allow an adult of reasonable muscle strength to generate considerable force with prolonged shaking. Caffey (1972) points out in his discussion of a child killed by his nursemaid that the baby had weighed 11 pounds. The nurse weighed 233 pounds, or 21 times the weight of the child. Caffey states, "Had the nurse been shaken by a caretaker of corresponding weight and strength, the monster would have weighed 21 times her weight or about . . . [5,000 pounds] and would have had the strength of 21 strong women."

Duhaime et al. (1987) constructed a biomechanical model of a 1-month-old infant and used an accelerometer to measure forces resulting from shaking injuries and impact injuries. They concluded that shaking alone could not generate sufficient force to cause serious head injuries in infants and that an impact with an object is necessary to produce injuries such as subdural hematomas and diffuse axonal injury. Alexander, Sato, Smith, and Bennett (1990) have disputed this model. They point out that children with evidence of impact injury were not more likely to die from their injuries than children without evidence of impact. Clinically, infants whose caretakers admit to shaking appear to have more global, serious, debilitating injury than children whose caretakers admit to hitting them on the head.

Several studies looking at injuries sustained by children who have fallen from beds and other short distances have concluded that short falls are not likely to cause serious head injuries in children, particularly when the history can be corroborated (Helfer, Slovis, & Black, 1977; Nimityongskul & Anderson, 1987; Williams, 1991).

TYPES OF INFANT HEAD INJURIES

The clinical spectrum of abusive infant head trauma can include the following types of injuries:

Injuries to the Scalp. Abrasions, lacerations, and bruising of the scalp are caused by direct blows. Infants with hemorrhage beneath the scalp may not show any lesions externally. The absence of obvious external scalp trauma does not rule out impact to the head.

Traumatic Alopecia (Hair Loss). When a child's hair is grabbed and pulled, spotty hair loss can occur. Initially, punctate bleeding and petechiae are noted at the site of hair loss. Boggy edema is sometimes palpated below areas of traumatic alopecia.

Subgaleal Hematomas (Bleeding Under the Scalp). The scalp is loosely attached to the skull via an aponeurosis. Disruption of the scalp can lead to extensive bleeding and even hypovolemic shock. Although extensive sub-galeal hematomas have been described after minor injuries to the head (Cooling & Viccellio, 1991; Kuban, Winston, & Bresnan, 1983), they can also occur after abusive head trauma.

Cephalohematomas (Bleeding Under the External Periosteum of the Skull). Cephalohematomas are common birth complications. We have seen three infants with the development of cephalohematomas, first noted at ages 2 to 4 months. It is unknown if these injuries were from birth trauma or acquired later. Cephalohematomas can be differentiated from subgaleal he-matomas on CT (computerized tomography) scans of the head. Cephalohe-matomas will not cross the suture lines of the infant's skull but end abruptly at sutures.

Skull Fractures. Accidental skull fractures are common injuries in tod-dlers. Most skull fractures caused by simple falls are uncomplicated, linear parietal fractures. Skull fractures resulting from abusive head trauma are more likely to be multiple or complex, depressed, or diastatic (wide) (Hobbs, 1984). Bilateral fractures and those crossing a suture line also are more likely to be associated with an abusive injury (Meservy, Towbin, McLaurin, Myers, & Ball, 1987).

Epidural Hematomas. Bleeding between the skull and the dura mater (a fibrous protective covering of the brain) is usually arterial bleeding, rapid, under pressure, and often life threatening. Epidural hematomas are rarely associated with child abuse injuries.

Dural Tears. Severe impact injuries can cause skull fractures with tearing of the dura mater. Blood, cerebrospinal fluid, and even brain tissue can extrude through the tear and into the subgaleal tissues beneath the scalp. These are serious injuries, requiring neurosurgical repair of the dura.

Subdural Hematomas. Subdural hematomas are a common complication of abuse head trauma from both impact and shaking. Delicate veins bridge the subdural space, draining into the venous sinuses formed from the dura. Traction from acceleration and deceleration causes these veins to tear. The classic lesion from abusive head trauma noted on CT and MRI (magnetic resonance imaging) of the head is subdural hematoma in the interhemispheric region along the falx cerebri (Harwood-Nash, 1992). MRI sometimes reveals hemorrhage and brain contusion not noted on CT (Alexander, Schor, & Smith, 1986) and is considered the procedure of choice when abusive head trauma is considered in the differential diagnosis (American Academy of Pediatrics, 1991).

Brain Tissue Injury. Shearing tears of the white matter (Calder, Hill, & Scholtz, 1984), diffuse axonal injury to the nerve cells (Vowles, Scholtz, & Cameron, 1987), and cerebral edema can result from shaking or impact head injuries. Anoxic brain damage often results from periods of respiratory compromise following these head injuries.

Spinal Cord Injury. Spinal cord injury at the junction of the cord and the brain stem has been found in infants who die of shaking injuries (Hadley, Sonntag, Rekate, & Murphy, 1989).

STUDY QUESTIONS

1. How common are head injuries as a form of child abuse?
2. How lethal is abusive head trauma?
3. What are the common patterns of head injury found in child abuse?

References

Alexander, R. C., Sato, Y., Smith, W., & Bennett, T. (1990). Incidence of impact trauma with cranial injuries ascribed to shaking. *American Journal of Diseases of Children, 144,* 724-726.

Alexander, R. C., Schor, D. P., & Smith, W. L. Jr. (1986). Magnetic resonance imaging of intracranial injuries from child abuse. *Journal of Pediatrics, 109,* 975-979.

American Academy of Pediatrics. Section on Radiology. (1991). Diagnostic imaging of child abuse. *Pediatrics, 87,* 262-264.

Caffey, J. (1946). Multiple fractures in the long bones of infants suffering from chronic subdural hematoma. *American Journal of Roentgenology, 56,* 163-173.

Caffey, J. (1972). On the theory and practice of shaking infants. *American Journal of Diseases of Children, 124,* 161-169.

Calder, I. M., Hill, I., & Scholtz, C. L. (1984). Primary brain trauma in non-accidental injury. *Journal of Clinical Pathology, 37,* 1095-1100.

Cooling, D. S., & Viccellio, P. (1991). Massive subgaleal hematoma following minor head trauma. *Journal of Emergency Medicine, 9,* Supplement 1, 33-35.

Duhaime, A. C., Gennarelli, T. A., Thibault, L. E., Bruce, D. A., Margulies, S. S., & Wiser, R. (1987). The shaken baby syndrome: A clinical, pathological, and biomechanical study. *Journal of Neurosurgery, 66,* 409-415.

Dykes, L. J. (1986). The whiplash shaken infant syndrome: What has been learned? *Child Abuse & Neglect, 10,* 211-221.

Hadley, M. N., Sonntag, V. K., Rekate, H. L., & Murphy, A. (1989). The infant whiplash-shake injury syndrome: A clinical and pathological study. *Neurosurgery, 24,* 586-540.

Harwood-Nash, D. C. (1992). Abuse to the pediatric central nervous system. *American Journal of Neuroradiology, 13,* 569-575.

Helfer, R. E., Slovis, T. L., Black, M. (1977). Injuries resulting when small children fall out of bed. *Pediatrics, 60,* 533-535.

Hobbs, C. J. (1984). Skull fracture and the diagnosis of abuse. *Archives of Diseases in Childhood, 59,* 246-252.

Kuban, K., Winston, K., & Bresnan, M. (1983). Childhood subgaleal hematoma following minor head trauma. *American Journal of Diseases of Children, 137,* 637-640.

Meservy, C. J., Towbin, R., McLaurin, R. L., Myers, P. A., & Ball, W. (1987). Radiographic characteristics of skull fractures resulting from child abuse. *American Journal of Roentgenology, 149,* 173-175.

Nimityongskul, P., & Anderson, L. D. (1987). The likelihood of injuries when children fall out of bed. *Journal of Pediatric Orthopedics, 7,* 184-186.

Sarsfield, J. K. (1974). The neurological sequelae of non-accidental injury. *Developmental Medicine in Child Neurology, 16,* 826-827.

Vowles, G. H., Scholtz, C. L., & Cameron, J. M. (1987). Diffuse axonal injury in early infancy. *Journal of Clinical Pathology, 40,* 185-189.

Williams, R. A. (1991). Injuries in infants and small children resulting from witnessed and corroborated free falls. *Journal of Trauma, 31,* 1350-1352.

8

Retinal Hemorrhages
and Other Eye Injuries

Basic References

> Budenz, D. L., Faber, M. G., Mirchandani, H. G., Park, H., & Rourke, L. B. (1994). Ocular and optic nerve hemorrhages in abused infants with intracranial injuries. *Ophthalmology, 101,* 559-565.

This elegant autopsy study documented optic nerve sheath hemorrhage as an important marker of trauma.

> Johnson, D. L., Braun, D., & Friendly, D. (1993). Accidental head trauma and retinal hemorrhage. *Neurosurgery, 33,* 231-234.

In this study, the authors compared retinal findings of accidental trauma to those of nonaccidental trauma. Retinal hemorrhage was rarely seen after accidental injury.

> Riffenburgh, R. S., & Sathyavagiswaran, L. (1991). Ocular findings at autopsy in child abuse victims. *Ophthalmology, 98,* 1519-1524.

This is a large autopsy study describing the changes seen after child abuse trauma.

Discussion

Retinal hemorrhages are a cardinal sign of abusive head trauma, or "shaken baby syndrome" (Riffenburgh & Sathyavagiswaran, 1991). The presence of retinal hemorrhage associated with subdural hematomas with or without associated injuries in a child under 2 years of age should be considered to be the result of child abuse until proven otherwise. The cause of these hemorrhages is not known, although several hypotheses have been suggested (Levin, 1990).

Four studies of retinal hemorrhages have shown them to be unusual in *accidental* head injuries. In one study (Duhaime et al., 1992), 100 consecutive head-injured children under 3 years old were prospectively examined. Ten children had retinal hemorrhages. Nine were abused, and 1 was a passenger in a high-speed motor vehicle accident who subsequently died of head injuries. In another prospective study of 79 head-injured children under 3 years old (Buys et al., 1992), 3 children had retinal hemorrhages, all of which were from nonaccidental trauma. A third prospective study of 25 nonintentionally head-injured children requiring hospital admission showed none to have retinal hemorrhages.

In a retrospective study (Johnson, Braun, & Friendly, 1993), 140 children with accidental head injuries were examined by an ophthalmologist, and 2 were found to have had retinal hemorrhages. Both children were involved in side-impact car accidents and sustained serious head injuries. The authors concluded that retinal hemorrhages were rarely found after nonintentional trauma in children.

In addition, these four studies strongly support the hypothesis that retinal hemorrhages do not occur after minor childhood injuries that do not involve substantial force.

Other injuries to the posterior segment of the eye also have been attributed to abusive shaking, impact head injuries in infants, or both. Preretinal hemorrhages are sometimes noted. These are large, ovoid hemorrhages found between the retinal internal limiting membrane (the layer of the retina closest to the center of the eye) and the retinal nerve fiber layer. They will often appear to be layered, with a fluid level noted at the top of the hemorrhage. These hemorrhages (also referred to as subhyaloid hemorrhages) are more accurately described by the pathologic term *intraretinal submembranous hemorrhage* (Yanoff & Fine, 1982). In addition to bleeding within the retinal layers, hemorrhage can occur within the vitreous of the eye (Greenwald, Weiss, Oesterle, & Friendly, 1986; Wilkinson, Han, Rappley, & Owings, 1989).

Other injuries include traumatic retinoschisis (separation of the layers of the retina) (Greenwald et al., 1986; Rho, Smith, Choi, Xu, & Kornblum, 1988), retinal detachment (Ober, 1980), and retinal folds around the macula (Massicotte, Folberg, Torczynski, Gilliland, & Luckenbach, 1991). The optic nerve itself may be damaged with bleeding into the optic nerve sheath (Lambert, Johnson, & Hoyt, 1986; Budenz, Faber, Mirchandi, Park, & Rourke, 1994) or even traumatic avulsion of the nerve off the back of the eye (R. A. King, personal communicaion, March 18, 1985).

Many victims of abusive head trauma will have partial or complete blindness or other visual deficits as a result of their trauma. Visual deficits may result from a dislocated lens (Levy et al., 1990), organization of vitreous hemorrhage, permanent retinal damage or detachment (Han & Wilkinson, 1990), or brain injury (Harcourt & Hopkins, 1971; Ludwig & Warman, 1984).

The differential diagnosis of retinal hemorrhages is extensive. Many of the causes of retinal hemorrhage listed in Table 8.1 have been reported only in adults or in a single case study and should be considered very rare causes of retinal hemorrhage. The presence of any one of these conditions does not rule out child abuse or shaken baby syndrome, especially when the child has other injuries. Many of the diseases and conditions that cause retinal hemorrhage in adults are not known to do the same in children, including hypertension and diabetes mellitus (Levin, 1990). Three conditions merit special consideration.

Retinal hemorrhages are commonly found in newborns after delivery (Bergen & Margolis, 1976). Risk factors for retinal hemorrhage with delivery include vacuum extraction (O'Leary, Ferrell, & Randolph, 1986), fetal distress, low weight for gestational age, low umbilical artery pH, and a short second stage of labor (Williams et al., 1993). Preterm infants are less likely than term infants to have retinal hemorrhages after delivery (Maltau, Egge, & Moe, 1984). Retinal hemorrhages in newborns have not been correlated with later developmental delays or strabismus (Bergen & Margolis, 1976; Levin et al., 1980). Most neonatal retinal hemorrhages resolve within 3 to 5 days, with a rare hemorrhage persisting up to 6 weeks (Selzen, 1970).

High altitude can also cause retinal hemorrhages. In one study, 4 of 14 climbers (28%) exposed to altitudes of 17,000 to 26,000 feet developed retinal hemorrhages (Butler, Harris, & Reynolds, 1992). In another study, 36% of climbers

TABLE 8.1 Causes of Retinal Hemorrhages Other Than Trauma

Environmental causes

Delivery of newborns (see text)	Resuscitation (see text)
High altitudes (see text)	Valsalva maneuver (Schipper, 1991)

Systemic diseases

Cystic fibrosis (Rimsza, Hernried, & Kaplan, 1978)	Malaria (Looareesuwan et al., 1983)
Diabetes mellitus (Dana et al., 1993)	Influenza (Weinberg & Nerney, 1983)
Sickle-cell disease (Dana et al., 1993)	Malignant melanoma (Lean & Gregor, 1980)
Hypertensive retinopathy (Dana et al., 1993)	Pancreatitis (Behrens-Baumann & Scheurer, 1991)
Rocky Mountain spotted fever (Sulewski & Green, 1986)	Leukemia
	Lymphoma
Osteogenesis imperfecta (Khalil, 1983)	Subacute bacterial endocarditis

Eye diseases

Retinal vein occlusion (Dana et al., 1993)	Congenital retinal dysplasia (Kaur & Taylor, 1992)
Macular degeneration (Dana et al., 1993)	Retinal detachment (Kaur & Taylor, 1992)
Persistent hyperplastic primary vitreous (Kaur & Taylor, 1992)	Retinal artery occlusion (Wallace et al., 1992)
Retinopathy of prematurity	Papilledema (Galvin & Sanders, 1980) (Kaur & Taylor, 1992)
Coat's disease (spontaneous retinal detachment, usually unilateral)	(Kaur & Taylor, 1992)

Cerebrovascular disease (Takano et al., 1992)

Intracranial aneurysms (McLellan, Prasad, & Punt, 1986)	Moyamoya disease (Takano et al., 1992)
Arteriovenous malformations (Takano et al., 1992)	Subarachnoid hemorrhage (Takano et al., 1992)

Hematologic diseases

Megaloblastic anemia (Lam & Lam, 1992)	Waldenstrom's macroglobulinemia (Goen & Terry, 1986)
von Willebrand's disease (Shiono et al., 1992)	G-6-PD deficiency (acute hemolytic crisis) (Sorcinelli & Guiso, 1979)
Thrombocytopenia (Frankel & Pastore, 1990)	Thrombasthenia (Glanzmann disease) (Vaiser et al., 1975)
Protein C deficiency (Peters et al., 1988)	Aplastic anemia (Lowenthal, Jones, & Desai, 1978)

exposed to altitudes above 14,200 feet developed hemorrhages (Shumacher & Petajan, 1975). Rapid ascent and strenuous exercise increased the likelihood of hemorrhage. Altitude stress is not likely to be a factor in cases of retinal hemorrhage in children because exposure to such altitudes is unlikely.

The most controversial cause of retinal hemorrhages in children is resuscitation. Postresuscitation hemorrhage has been documented in children with severe asthma, near drowning, sudden infant death syndrome (Goetting & Sowa, 1990; Kirschner & Stein, 1985), aspiration (Bacon, Sayer, & Howe, 1978), fatal burns (Weedn, Mansour, & Nichols, 1990), and fatal dehydration (Kramer & Goldstein, 1993). However, an attempt to create retinal hemorrhages in an animal after resuscitation of newborn piglets was unsuccessful despite the generation of high sagittal sinus and atrial pressures (Fackler, Berkowitz, & Green, 1992). In two prospective studies, retinal hemorrhages were seen in 2% and 10% of resuscitated children without preceding trauma when examined by direct ophthalmoscopy. Therefore, retinal hemorrhages are not a common finding after resuscitation (Goetting & Sowa, 1990; Kanter, 1986).

Most causes of retinal hemorrhage other than trauma are easily ruled out by a history, physical examination, and a few readily available laboratory tests. One confusing aspect of the terminology involved in describing the origin of intraocular hemorrhage is the use of the term *Terson's syndrome*. Originally, Terson's syndrome described the vitreous hemorrhage that often occurred with subarachnoid hemorrhage (Williams, Mieler, & Williams, 1990). The term has gradually evolved to describe intraocular hemorrhages occurring because of rapid changes in intracranial pressure leading to retinal venous hypertension (Kahn & Frenkel, 1975). Although changes in intracranial pressure can lead to retinal hemorrhages, the underlying cause of those hemorrhages in children is most often trauma or, more specifically, nonaccidental trauma. It is inadequate to attribute hemorrhages to intracranial pressure changes in the absence of an underlying disease or condition.

Another confusing term is *Purtscher's retinopathy*, retinal hemorrhages and exudates following severe, abrupt chest compression. Purtscher's retinopathy is commonly seen after chest compression from vehicles rolling over the chest or from compression by a seat belt during automobile accidents (Kelley, 1973). It has also been reported in battered babies who do not have subdural hematomas (Tomasi & Rosman, 1975), implying optic injury from increased intrathoracic pressure without associated head injury.

The list of causes of retinal hemorrhages includes many diseases associated with blood dyscrasias, platelet deficiencies, or severe anemia. Neither anemia nor thrombocytopenia alone should cause retinal hemorrhages. However, the two combined can cause retinal hemorrhage; when hemoglobin is less than 8 gm/dl and platelets are less than 100,000/mm (Duhaime et al.,

TABLE 8.2 Eye Injuries Caused by Nonaccidental Trauma

Cataracts (Friendly, 1971)	Cornea burns (Olver & Hague, 1989)
Dislocated lenses (Friendly, 1971)	Subconjunctival hemorrhage (Olver & Hague, 1989)
Hyphema (Friendly, 1971)	Corneal edema (Tseng & Keys, 1976)
Lid lacerations (Friendly, 1971)	Elevated intraocular pressure (Tseng & Keys, 1976)
Periorbital edema (Friendly, 1971)	Sixth-nerve palsy (Harley, 1980)
Periorbital ecchymoses (Friendly, 1971)	Chemical eye injury (Taylor & Bentovim, 1976)
Traumatic uveitis (Hendeles, Barber, & Willshaw, 1985)	Tarsorrhaphy secondary to the use of cyanoacrylate adhesives (Blinder, Scott, & Lange, 1987)
Canthus burns (Olver & Hague, 1989)	

1992) at the same time, retinal hemorrhages may occur in 70% of patients (Yanoff & Fine, 1982).

In summary, nonaccidental trauma is a common cause of retinal hemorrhages in children. When retinal hemorrhages are noted in the absence of a significant trauma history, an examination by an ophthalmologist will be helpful in ruling out organic disease. A CT scan or MRI scan should also be conducted to look for intracranial pathology. Most important, the diagnosis of nonaccidental trauma should be considered and investigated to protect the safety of the child.

In regard to other types of opthalmic trauma from child abuse, one series showed that 4 of 133 children presented to an eye clinic for emergency injury treatment were abused children. A wide spectrum of eye injuries have been attributed to child abuse. Table 8.2 lists types of injuries described in the literature.

STUDY QUESTIONS

1. Retinal hemorrages are considered a cardinal sign of what child abuse trauma?

2. Give a differential diagnosis of retinal hemorrhages.

3. Describe the spectrum of eye injuries found in child abuse.

References

Bacon, C. J., Sayer, G. C., & Howe, J. W. (1978). Extensive retinal hemorrhages in infancy: An innocent cause. *British Medical Journal, 1*, 281.

Behrens-Baumann, W., & Scheurer, G. (1991). Morbus Purtscher: Variationsbreite der klinischen Manifestationen bei 11 Patienten und Uberlegungen zur Pathogenese. *Klinische Monatsblätter Für Augenheilkunde und Augenärztliche Fortbildung, 198*, 99-107.

Bergen, R., & Margolis, S. (1976). Retinal hemorrhages in the newborn. *Annals of Ophthalmology, 8*, 53-56.

Blinder, K. J., Scott, W., & Lange, M. P. (1987). Abuse of cyanoacrylate in child abuse: Case report. *Archives of Ophthalmology, 105*, 1632-1633.

Budenz, D. L., Faber, M. G., Mirchandi, H. G., Park, H., & Rourke, L. B. (1994). Ocular and optic nerve hemorrhages in abused infants with intracranial injuries. *Ophthalmology, 101*, 559-565.

Butler, F. K., Harris, D. J. Jr., & Reynolds, R. D. (1992). Altitude retinopathy on Mount Everest, 1989. *Ophthalmology, 99*, 739-746.

Buys, Y. M., Levin, A. V., Enzenauer, R. W., Elder, J. E., Letourneau, M. A., Humphreys, R. P., Mian, M., & Morin, J. D. (1992). Retinal findings after head trauma in infants and young children. *Ophthalmology, 99*, 1718-1723.

Dana, M. R., Werner, M. S., Viana, M. A., & Shapiro, M. J. (1993). Spontaneous and traumatic vitreous hemorrhage. *Ophthalmology, 100*, 1377-1383.

Duhaime, A. C., Alario, A. J., Lewander, W. J., Schut, L., Sutton, L. N., Loporchia, S., Seidl, T. S., Nudelman, S., Budenz, D., Hertle, R., & Tsiaras, W. (1992). Head injury in very young children: Mechanisms, injury types, and ophthalmologic findings in 100 hospitalized patients younger than 2 years of age. *Pediatrics, 90*, 179-185.

Fackler, J. C., Berkowitz, I. D., & Green, W. R. (1992). Retinal hemorrhages in newborn piglets following cardiopulmonary resuscitation. *American Journal of Diseases of Children, 146*, 1294-1296.

Frankel, C. A., & Pastore, D. J. (1990). Idiopathic thrombocytopenic purpura with intracranial hemorrhage and vitreous hemorrhage. *Clinical Pediatrics (Philadelphia), 29*, 725-728.

Friendly, D. S. (1971). Ocular manifestations of physical child abuse. *Transactions of the American Academy of Ophthalmology and Otolaryngology, 75*, 318-332.

Galvin, R., & Sanders, M. D. (1980). Peripheral retinal hemorrhages with papilloedema. *British Journal of Ophthalmology, 64*, 262-266.

Goen, T. M., & Terry, J. E. (1986). Mid-peripheral hemorrhages secondary to Waldenstrom's macroglobulinemia. *Journal of American Optomology Association, 57*, 109-112.

Goetting, M. G., & Sowa, B. (1990). Retinal hemorrhage after cardiopulmonary resuscitation in children: An etiologic reevaluation. *Pediatrics, 85*, 585-588.

Greenwald, M. J., Weiss, A., Oesterle, C. S., & Friendly, D. S. (1986). Traumatic retinoschisis in battered babies. *Ophthalmology, 93,* 618-625.

Han, D. P., & Wilkinson, W. S. (1990). Late ophthalmic manifestations of the shaken baby syndrome. *Journal of Pediatric Ophthalmology and Strabismus, 27,* 299-303.

Harcourt, B., & Hopkins, D. (1971). Ophthalmic manifestations of the battered-baby syndrome. *British Medical Journal, 3,* 398-401.

Harley, R. D. (1980). Ocular manifestations of child abuse. *Journal of Pediatric Ophthalmology and Strabismus, 17,* 5-13.

Hendeles, S., Barber, K., & Willshaw, H. E. (1985). The risk of ocular involvement in non-accidental injury. *Child Care, Health, and Development, 11,* 345-348.

Hymel, K. P., & Jenny, C. (1996). Abusive spiral fractures of the humerus: A videotapted exception. *Archives of Pediatrics and Adolescent Medicine, 150,* 226-228.

Johnson, D. L., Braun, D., & Friendly, D. (1993). Accidental head trauma and retinal hemorrhage. *Neurosurgery, 33,* 231-234.

Kahn, S. G., & Frenkel, M. (1975). Intravitreal hemorrhage associated with rapid increase in intracranial pressure (Terson's Syndrome). *American Journal of Ophthalmology, 80,* 37-43.

Kanter, R. K. (1986). Retinal hemorrhage after cardiopulmonary resuscitation or child abuse. *Journal of Pediatrics, 108,* 430-432.

Kaur, B., & Taylor, D. (1992). Fundus hemorrhages in infancy. *Survey of Ophthalmology, 37,* 1-17.

Kelley, J. S. (1973). Purtscher's retinopathy related to chest compression by safety belts: Fluorescein angiographic findings. *American Journal Ophthalmology, 74,* 278-283.

Khalil, M. K. (1983). Subhyaloid hemorrhage in osteogenesis imperfecta tarda. *Canadian Journal of Ophthalmology, 18,* 251-252.

Kirschner, R. H., & Stein, R. J. (1985). The mistaken diagnosis of child abuse: A form of medical abuse? *American Journal of Diseases of Children, 139,* 873-875.

Kramer, K., & Goldstein, B. (1993). Retinal hemorrhages following cardiopulmonary resuscitation. *Clinical Pediatrics (Philadelphia), 33,* 366-368.

Lam, S., & Lam, B. L. (1992). Bilateral retinal hemorrhages from megaloblastic anemia: Case report and review of literature. *Annals of Ophthalmology, 24,* 86-90.

Lambert, S. R., Johnson, T. E., & Hoyt, C. S. (1986). Optic nerve sheath and retinal hemorrhages associated with the shaken baby syndrome. *Archives of Ophthalmology, 104,* 1509-1512.

Lean, J. S., & Gregor, Z. (1980). The acute vitreous hemorrhage. *British Journal of Ophthalmology, 64,* 469-471.

Levin, A. V. (1990). Ocular manifestations of child abuse. *Ophthalmology Clinic, North America, 3,* 249-264.

Levin, S., Janive, J., Mintz, M., Kreisler, C., Romem, M., Klutznik, A., Feingold, M., & Insler, V. (1980). Diagnostic and prognostic value of retinal hemorrhages in the neonate. *Obstetrics and Gynecology, 55,* 309-314.

Levy, I., Wysenbeek, Y. S., Nitzan, M., Nissenkorn, I., Lerman-Sagle, T., & Steinherz, R. (1990). Occult ocular damage as a leading sign in the battered child syndrome. *Metabolic, Pediatric, and Systematic Ophthalmology, 13,* 20-22.

Looareesuwan, S., Warrell, D. A., White, N. J., Chanthavanich, P., Warrell, M. J., Chantaratherakitti, S., Changswek, S., Chongmankongcheep, L., & Kanchanaranya, C. (1983). Retinal hemorrhage, a common sign of prognostic significance in cerebral malaria. *American Journal of Tropical Medicine and Hygiene, 32,* 911-915.

Lowenthal, M. N., Jones, I. G., & Desai, M. (1978). Aplastic anaemia and optic fundus hemorrhages due to traditional herbal remedies. *American Journal of Tropical Medicine and Hygiene, 81,* 177-179.

Ludwig, S., & Warman, M. (1984). Shaken baby syndrome: a review of 20 cases. *Annals of Emergency Medicine, 13,* 104-107.

Maltau, J. M., Egge, K., & Moe, N. (1984). Retinal hemorrhages in the preterm neonate: A prospective randomized study comparing the occurrence of hemorrhages after spontaneous versus forceps delivery. *Acta Obstetrica et Gynecolica, Scandinavica, 63,* 219-221.

Massicotte, S. J., Folberg, R., Torczynski, E., Gilliland, M. G., & Luckenbach, M. W. (1991). Vitreoretinal traction and perimacular retinal folds in the eyes of deliberately traumatized children. *Ophthalmology, 98,* 1124-1127.

McLellan, N. J., Prasad, R., & Punt, J. (1986). Spontaneous subhyaloid and retinal hemorrhages in an infant. *Archives of Diseases in Childhood, 61,* 1130-1132.

Ober, R. R. (1980). Hemorrhagic retinopathy in infancy: A clinicopathologic report. *Journal of Pediatric Ophthalmology and Strabismus, 17,* 17-20.

O'Leary, J. A., Ferrell, R. E., & Randolph, C. R. (1986). Retinal hemorrhage and vacuum extraction delivery. *Journal of Perinatal Medicine, 14,* 197-199.

Olver, J. M., & Hague, S. (1989). Children presenting to an ophthalmic casualty department. *Eyes, 3,* 415-419.

Peters, C., Casella, J. F., Marlar, R. A., Montgomery, R. R., & Zinkham, W. H. (1988). Homozygous protein C deficiency: Observations on the nature of the molecular abnormality and the effectiveness of warfarin therapy. *Pediatrics, 81,* 272-276.

Rho, N., Smith, R. E., Choi, J. H., Xu, X. H., & Kornblum, R. N. (1988). Autopsy findings in the eyes of fourteen fatally abused children. *Forensic Science International, 39,* 293-299.

Riffenburgh, R. S., Sathyavagiswaran, L. (1991). Ocular findings at autopsy in child abuse victims. *Ophthalmology, 98,* 1519-1524.

Rimsza, M. E., Hernried, L. S., & Kaplan, A. M. (1978). Hemorrhagic retinopathy in a patient with cystic fibrosis. *Pediatrics, 62,* 336-338.

Schipper, I. (1991). Valsalvamanover: nicht immer gutartig. *Klinische Monatsblaetter Fuer Augenheilkunde und Augenarztliche Fortbildung, 198,* 457-459.

Selzen, F. (1970). Retinal hemorrhages in newborn infants. *British Journal of Ophthalmology, 55,* 248-253.

Shiono, T., Abe, S., Watabe, T., Noro, M., Tamai, M., Akutsu, Y., Ishikawa, M., Suzuki, S., & Mori, K. (1992). Vitreous, retinal, and subretinal hemorrhages associated with von Willebrand's syndrome. *Graefe's Archive for Clinical Experimental Ophthalmology, 230*, 496-497.

Shumacher, G. A., & Petajan, J. H. (1975). High-altitude stress and retinal hemorrhage: Relation to vascular headache mechanisms. *Archives of Environmental Health, 30*, 217-221.

Sorcinelli, R., & Guiso, G. (1979). Vitreoretinal hemorrhages after ingestion of fava beans in a G-6-PD-deficient subject. *Ophthalmologica, 178*, 259-262.

Sulewski, M. E., & Green, W. R. (1986). Ocular histopathologic features of a presumed case of Rocky Mountain spotted fever. *Retina, 6*, 125-130.

Takano, S., Saito, M., Miyasaka, Y., Yada, K., Kitahara, T., Ohwada, T., & Takagi, H. (1992). Fundus hemorrhage in patients with intracranial hemorrhage caused by cerebrovascular disease: Its clinical significance. *Brain and Nerve, 44*, 13-17.

Taylor, D., & Bentovim, A. (1976). Recurrent nonaccidentally inflicted chemical eye injuries to siblings. *Journal of Pediatric Ophthalmology, 13*, 238-242.

Tomasi, L. G., & Rosman, N. P. (1975). Purtscher retinopathy in the battered child syndrome. *American Journal of Diseases of Children, 129*, 1335-1337.

Tseng, S. S., & Keys, M. P. (1976). Battered child syndrome simulating congenital glaucoma. *Archives of Ophthalmology, 94*, 839-840.

Vaiser, A., Hutton, W. L., Marengo-Rowe, A. J., Leveson, J. E., & Snyder, W. B. (1975). Retinal hemorrhage associated with thrombasthenia. *American Journal of Ophthalmology, 80*, 258-262.

Wallace, R. T., Brown, G. C., Benson, W., & Sivalingham A. (1992). Sudden retinal manifestations of intranasal cocaine and methamphetamine abuse. *American Journal of Ophthalmology, 114*, 158-160.

Weedn, V. W., Mansour, A. M., & Nichols, M. M. (1990). Retinal hemorrhage in an infant after cardiopulmonary resuscitation. *American Journal of Forensic Medicine and Pathology, 11*, 79-82.

Weinberg, R. J., & Nerney, J. J. (1983). Bilateral submacular hemorrhages associated with an influenza syndrome. *Annals of Ophthalmology, 15*, 710-712.

Wilkinson, W. S., Han, D. P., Rappley, M. D., & Owings, C. L. (1989). Retinal hemorrhage predicts neurologic injury in shaken baby syndrome. *Archives of Ophthalmology, 107*, 1472-1474.

Williams, D. F., Mieler, W. F., & Williams, G. A. (1990). Posterior segment manifestations of ocular trauma. *Retina, 10*, S35-S44.

Williams, M. C., Knuppel, R. A., O'Brien, W. F., Weiss, A., Spellacy, W. N., & Pietrantoni, M. (1993). Obstetric correlates of neonatal retinal hemorrhage. *Obstetrics and Gynecology, 81*, 688-694.

Yanoff, M., & Fine, B. S. (1982). *Ocular pathology* (pp. 498, 601-603). Philadelphia: Harper & Row.

Injuries to the Skin

Basic References

Brown, J., & Melinkovich, P. (1986). Schönlein-Henoch purpura misdiagnosed as suspected child abuse. *Journal of the American Medical Association, 256,* 617-618.

In addition to the discussion of an unusual case, the authors review the literature on lesions confused with bruising.

DiMaio, D. J., & DiMaio, V. J. M. (1989). *Forensic pathology* (pp. 87-108). New York: Elsevier.

This chapter gives an excellent overview of the pathology and mechanisms of injury in blunt trauma.

Ellerstein, N. S. (1979). The cutaneous manifestations of child abuse and neglect. *American Journal of Diseases of Children, 133,* 906-909.

Ellerstein's article is an often-quoted classic.

Frechette, A., Rimsza, M. E. (1992). Stun gun injury: A new presentation of the battered child syndrome. *Pediatrics, 89,* **898-901.**

As in the Brown article, this article uses a clinical case as a starting point to discuss circular skin lesions. On page 900 is an excellent table describing the differential diagnosis.

Johnson, C. F. (1990). Inflicted injury versus accidental injury. *Pediatric Clinics of North America, 37,* **791-814.**

Although this article addresses issues beyond skin injury, it is one of the best reviews of the manifold presentations of skin trauma in abused children.

Wagner, G. N. (1986). Bitemark identification in child abuse cases. *Pediatric Dentistry, 8,* **96-100.**

This article contains everything a generalist needs to know about bite-marks.

Wedgwood, J. (1990). Childhood bruising. *Practitioner, 234,* **598-601.**

This study is simple, elegant and profound. The authors address a commonly encountered pediatric question and reach the conclusion that bruising in small infants in almost always inflicted.

Discussion

PREVALENCE OF INJURIES TO THE SKIN

Skin lesions are commonly identified on abused children, as well as on normal children. One study showed 37% of *normal* children, age 2 weeks to 11 years, to have bruises and abrasions on their body (Roberton, Barbor, & Hull, 1982). In this study, Roberton and colleagues observed 400 children presented for routine medical care. They compared the skin lesions in this group with the skin lesions found in 84 cases of suspected child abuse. Several interesting conclusions were reached. Injuries were very uncommon in children under 9 months of age. They increased in frequency until 3 years of age, the group with the highest prevalence of injury. Superficial injuries to the head and face were most common in toddlers and uncommon in older children. Injuries to the lumbar region were not seen before 3 years of age. All injuries were more common in abused children than in normal children, but the greatest disparity was found with injuries to the head and face, followed by injuries to the thighs and buttocks.

Wedgwood (1990) studied the prevalence of bruises on children related to their motor abilities. He found that children who could not yet cruise holding onto furniture had no bruises whatsoever. The number of bruises increased with increasing motor skills, with children who walked up stairs without alternating their feet having the most bruises. Once children had enough motor competence to alternate their feet when walking up stairs, the number of bruises they sustained decreased.

DEFINITIONS OF SKIN TRAUMA
AND PATHOLOGICAL MECHANISMS

Contusions

Contusions (bruises) are an area of hemorrhage into soft tissue due to the rupture of blood vessels caused by blunt trauma. The severity of contusions depends on the force applied to the tissue and the nature and vascularity of the tissue itself. With severe beating, blood loss into the tissues may be severe enough to cause hypovolemic shock (Eichelberger, Beal, & May, 1991).

When an object hits the skin, the tissue may deform and capillary bleeding may occur at the edges of the object, sparing the center (Johnson, 1990). Thus, it is not uncommon for marks left by slapping with a hand to display the outline of the fingers.

Many skin lesions can be confused with child abuse bruises, including postmortem livor (DiMaio & DiMaio, 1989), Schönlein-Henoch purpura (Brown & Melinkovich, 1986), coagulopathies, disseminated intravascular coagulation, purpura fulminans, hypersensitivity vasculitis, erythema multiformae, and Mongolian spots (Kirschner & Stein, 1985).

As bruises fade, color changes will occur, representing the metabolisms and transport of iron containing pigments found in blood cells (Wilson, 1977). Many factors influence the time required of healing, including the blood supply of the tissues and the depth of the injury. Although it is reasonable to conclude that injuries are old or recent, giving the exact length of time since the occurrence of injury based on color alone is not likely to be accurate.

A common finding in child abuse cases is multiple bruises of different ages, implying ongoing injury (Ellerstein, 1979). The shape of bruises will sometimes reflect the object used to inflict the injury.

Abrasions

Abrasions are injuries to the skin causing the most superficial layer of skin cell (epidermis) to be removed (DiMaio & DiMaio, 1989). Three types of abrasions occur. *Brush abrasions* are caused by blunt objects scraping off skin cells. Common examples are scraped knees from sliding on concrete, and scratches. Dragging a child across a rough surface can also cause brush abrasions. *Impact abrasions* are caused by blunt objects directly impacting the skin and crushing it. *Pattern abrasions* are impact abrasions where an imprint of the offending object is left. Beating a child with a looped cord or a stick will often leave a pattern abrasion, as well as bruises.

Lacerations

Lacerations are tears in tissue caused by shearing or crushing (DiMaio & DiMaio, 1989). The pattern of a laceration does not necessarily reflect the shape of the object that caused it. If the blow causing the laceration is delivered at an angle, the edges of the wound will be undermined on one side and beveled on the other. Lacerations are more likely to be found over bony prominence where skin is fixed to underlying tissue.

Other Skin Lesions

Bitemarks. Bitemarks are sometimes encountered in child abuse cases (Wagner, 1986). They must be carefully evaluated and documented, including swabbing fresh bitemarks for saliva evidence and photographing with and without size standards. Forensic dental consultation is important in maximizing the evidentiary usefulness of bitemarks. Skin injuries from defibrillation during resuscitation have been confused with bitemarks (Grey, 1989).

Masque Ecchymotique. Masque ecchymotique is a condition sometimes caused by child abuse (Perrot, 1989). Its signs are cervicofacial cyanosis, subconjunctival hemorrhage, and severe vascular engorgement and ecchymoses of the face and neck. The symptom complex has been related to crush injuries of the thorax. Another mechanism that has been noted in a child abuse case (Perrot, 1989) is an accordion type of pressure caused by holding the child by the buttocks and neck and forcefully flexing the trunk.

Stun Gun Injuries. Stun gun injuries create a pattern of paired round lesions, about 0.5 cm in diameter approximately 5.0 cm apart. Frechette and Rimsza (1992) reported a case of stun gun injury to an abused child.

Tattoos and Symbolic Abrasions or Lacerations of the Skin. Children can be abusively marked with tattoos or other ritualistic or symbolic marks (Johnson, 1994). Tattooing involves the injection of permanent dye under the skin.

Folk Medicine Practices. Some folk medicine practices can cause lesions that can be confused with child abuse (Feldman, 1984; Yeatman & Dang, 1980). The two most commonly cited are *moxibustion* and *cao gio.* Moxibustion is the burning of herbs on the child's skin to rid the child of illness. Cao gio is the rubbing of the child's chest with a heated coin or spoon, causing linear, inflamed streaks on the skin.

Constricting Bands. Constricting bands can cause abusive injury when applied to a child's hands, feet, digits, or penis (Johnson, 1988).

STUDY QUESTIONS

1. What are the common "pattern injuries" that occur in abused children, based on the object with which the child was hit?

2. What are the patterns and numbers of bruises that occur commonly on nonabused children, based on age and developmental level?

References

Brown, J., & Melinkovich, P. (1986). Schönlein-Henoch purpura misdiagnosed as suspected child abuse. *Journal of American Medical Association, 256,* 617-618.

DiMaio, D. J., & DiMaio, V. J. M. (1989). *Forensic pathology* (pp. 87-108). New York: Elsevier.

Eichelberger. S. P., Beal, D. W., & May, R. B. (1991). Hypovolemic shock in a child as a consequence of corporal punishment. *Pediatrics, 87,* 570-571.

Ellerstein, N. S. (1979). The cutaneous manifestations of child abuse and neglect. *American Journal of Diseases of Children, 133,* 906-909.

Feldman, D. W. (1984). Pseudoabusive burns in Asian refugees. *American Journal of Diseases of Children, 138,* 768-769.

Frechette, A., & Rimsza, M. E. (1992). Stun gun injury: A new presentation of the battered child syndrome. *Pediatrics, 89,* 898-901.

Grey, T. C. (1989). Defibrillator injury suggesting bitemark. *American Journal of Forensic Medicine and Pathology, 10,* 144-145.

Johnson, C. F. (1988). Constricting bands: Manifestations of possible child abuse. *Clinical Pediatrics (Philadelphia), 27,* 439-444.

Johnson, C. F. (1990). Inflicted injury versus accidental injury. *Pediatric Clinic, North America, 37,* 791-814.

Johnson, C. F. (1994). Symbolic scarring and tattooing. *Clinical Pediatrics (Philadelphia), 33,* 46-49.

Kirschner, R. H., & Stein, R. J. (1985). The mistaken diagnosis of child abuse. A form of medical abuse? *American Journal of Diseases of Children, 139,* 873-875.

Perrot, L. J. (1989). Masque ecchymotique: Specific or nonspecific indicator for abuse. *American Journal of Forensic Medicine and Pathology, 10,* 95-97.

Roberton, D. M., Barbor, P., & Hull, D. (1982). Unusual injury? Recent injury in normal children and children with suspected non-accidental injury. *British Medical Journal, 285,* 1399-1401.

Wagner, G. N. (1986). Bitemark identification in child abuse cases. *Pediatric Dentistry, 8,* 96-100.

Wedgwood, J. (1990). Childhood bruising. *Practitioner, 234,* 598-601.

Wilson, E. F. (1977). Estimation of the age of cutaneous contusions in child abuse. *Pediatrics, 60,* 750-752.

Yeatman, G. W., & Dang, V. V. (1980). Cao gio (coin rubbing). *Journal of the American Medical Association, 244,* 2748-2749.

Child Sexual Abuse

Epidemiology, Risk Factors, and Evaluation

Basic References

Finkelhor, D. (1986). *A sourcebook on child sexual abuse.* Beverly Hills, CA: Sage.

This comprehensive text reviews epidemiological and sociological aspects of child sexual abuse.

Finkelhor, D. (1993). Epidemiological factors in the clinical identification of child sexual abuse. *Child Abuse & Neglect, 17,* 67-70.

This article provides a thoughtful review of various risk factors and statistical facts about child sexual abuse.

Giardino, A. P., Finkel, M. A., Giardino, E. R., Seidl, T., & Ludwig, S. (1992). *A practical guide to the evaluation of sexual abuse in the prepubertal child.* Newbury Park, CA: Sage.

As the name implies, this book provides an extremely practical approach to sexual abuse evaluation.

> **Heger, A., & Emans, S. J. (1992).** *Evaluation of the sexually abused child: A medical textbook and photographic atlas.* **New York: Oxford University Press.**

This is a comprehensive text on the medical aspects of sexual abuse, which includes a thorough treatment of the evaluation process.

> **Leventhal, J. M. (1988). Have there been changes in the epidemiology of sexual abuse of children during the 20th century?** *Pediatrics, 82*(5), **766-773.**

This article compares Kinsey's data from the earlier 20th century with more recent studies of the prevalence of sexual abuse to examine trends in the occurrence of abuse.

> **Russell, D. E. H. (1984).** *Sexual exploitation: Rape, child sexual abuse, and workplace harassment.* **Beverly Hills, CA: Sage.**

Dr. Russell reports on large-scale epidemiological studies she has conducted on the prevalence and seriousness of sexual crimes against women and children.

Discussion

PREVALENCE AND RISK FACTORS
FOR CHILD SEXUAL ABUSE

Sexual abuse is commonly experienced by children. The National Incidence Study conducted by the National Center on Child Abuse and Neglect (1981) during 1979 to 1980 reported an incidence of sexual abuse reported to authorities to be 0.7 per 1,000 children. Because many cases are not reported, this figure is lower than the actual number of children being abused. Prevalence rates of adults reporting sexual abuse as children vary from 6% to 62% in women and 3% to 30% in men, depending on the definition and sampling techniques used and the population studied (Finkelhor, 1993).

Reports of child sexual abuse to social service agencies have been increasing steadily over the last 20 years. Research by Russell and Leventhal would suggest that the incidence of child sexual abuse is actually increasing and that the increase in reports of abuse is not due to greater societal awareness of the problem alone (Leventhal, 1988).

Several risk factors for sexual abuse have been identified. Girls are more likely to be abused than boys, although boys may be less likely to report abuse. Children are more likely to be abused in the preadolescent years, ages 8 to 12. Other children who are more likely to be at risk are those from socially isolated families, those with absent or unavailable parents, and those who grow up in families with a nonbiologically related father or father figure in the home (stepfather or mother's boyfriend). Race and social class have not been shown consistently to be risk factors for sexual abuse (Finkelhor, 1993).

For the medical practitioner, prevalence data indicate that sexual abuse is a very common and pervasive problem. The ability to recognize, diagnose, and treat sexual abuse in medical practice is crucial for the promotion of health of children.

STUDY QUESTIONS

1. What is the epidemiology of child sexual abuse?
2. What are some of the risk factors that have been identified for child sexual abuse?

EVALUATION OF CHILDREN IN
CASES OF SUSPECTED SEXUAL ABUSE

After an acute assault, forensic evidence of semen may persist for several days (Kanda, Thomas, & Lloyd, 1985). The chances of recovering useful evidence, however, are slight after 72 hours. The persistence of evidence depends on the nature of the assault, the age of the child, the orifices assaulted (vaginal sperm persist longer than rectal or oral sperm), and the activities of the child after the assault. Bathing or brushing teeth can quickly remove any evidence of contact with semen.

Children who call or visit a medical facility reporting sexual abuse or assault may not need immediate medical examination (Seidel, Elvik, Berkowitz, & Day, 1986). An evaluation should be done immediately if the following occurs:

1. The child has had sexual contact within 72 hours of the report.

2. The child has injuries that should be treated, documented, or both. Genital and anal injuries in children heal quickly and may not persist if the examination is delayed.

3. The child is ill or injured or has symptoms of vaginal or anal discharge or bleeding. These children can be triaged for immediate care or care within a few days, depending on the nature of the symptoms.

4. The child reports depression or suicidal ideation.

5. The person taking the report ascertains the child to be in immediate danger of reabuse or reprisal by the perpetrator. The child can be brought to the emergency department for safety until the authorities have been contacted.

STUDY QUESTION

3. In general, should children reporting sexual abuse undergo a medical examination? Under what circumstances should an examination be performed immediately?

In general, the medical examination will probably be less difficult for the child if it is *not* performed in the emergency department (Smith, Losek, Glaeser, & Walsh-Kelly, 1988). A clinic visit for examination by a skilled examiner would be preferable. However, any child or family reporting abuse will need support and comfort. This can sometimes be done by a phone contact or a visit with the hospital social worker. Also, enough data must be gathered immediately to report the abuse to the proper authorities.

Some children may not report vaginal, anal, or oral penetration. A child who has been externally fondled may not need medical evaluation. However, many children will minimize their experiences or be embarrassed to disclose penetrating injury. In addition, children who do not have genital penetration can still contract sexually transmitted diseases, such as gonorrhea. Generally, all children reporting sexual abuse should have a medical examination by a trained examiner, if this service is available (Gallagher, 1993).

One function of the medical examination is to allay the child's fears about being injured or "different" from other children. Many sexually abused children will express concerns about their ability to marry and have children as adults. A medical examiner can reassure a child that she or he is physically healthy and normal (Berkowitz, 1987).

Signs and Symptoms of
Sexual Abuse of Children

Many behavioral signs of sexual abuse are similar to those experienced by children who suffer from posttraumatic stress disorder (McLeer, Deblinger, Atkins, Foa, & Ralphe, 1988). Most physical symptoms are not specific to sexual abuse but can be seen in other medical illnesses as well (Hunter, Kilstrom, & Loda, 1985; Krugman, 1986). Table 10.1 lists common signs and symptoms identified in sexually abused children.

Children are more likely to present to an outpatient clinic signs or symptoms of abuse rather than specific complaints of abuse. Recognizing the presenting problem as a manifestation of abuse requires a high "index of suspicion" and a knowledge of the signs and symptoms of abuse.

Sexual acting-out behavior is very common in abused children. Although interest in the opposite sex, masturbation, and touching one's own sexual organs are common behaviors in children, aggressive sexual behavior or overt imitation of sexual acts are uncommon in normal, non-abused children (Friedrich, Grambsch, Broughton, Kuiper, & Beilke, 1991).

Obtaining a History From
Children in a Medical Setting

It is important to coordinate interviewing with other professionals to minimize trauma to the child. Limiting the number of interviews with a child is a worthwhile goal. In some communities, a single interview suffices for all professionals, including police, prosecutors and social workers (Jones & McQuiston, 1984). In other jurisdictions, physicians are encouraged to repeat interviews because of the value of physician testimony in court. Also, physicians may be able to obtain information during the physical examination that others have not obtained. Physicians, law enforcement officers, prosecutors, and social service workers should work together to coordinate services in each community, depending on that community's needs and resources.

There are many different approaches to interviewing children when sexual abuse is suspected. Most authors agree, however, on certain principles that must be followed because of the medical and legal implications of the interview (MacFarlane & Krebs, 1986).

TABLE 10.1 Presentations of Sexual Abuse

Early warnings
  General statements about abuse
  Sexualized play
Direct statements about abuse
  Behavioral changes
  Sleep disturbances
  Appetite disturbances
  Neurotic or conduct disorders
  Phobias, avoidance behavior
  Withdrawal, depression
  Guilt
  Temper tantrums, aggressive behavior
  Excessive masturbation
  Suicidal behavior
  Hysterical or conversion reactions
Medical conditions
  Genital, anal, or urethra trauma
  Genital infection
  Sexually transmitted diseases
  Recurrent urinary tract infections
  Abdominal pain
  Chronic genital or anal pain
  Enuresis
  Encopresis
Other problems
  Pregnancy
  School problems
  Promiscuity/prostitution
  Substance abuse
  Sexual perpetration to others

SOURCE: Adapted from Krugman (1986, p. 28).

Establishing a relationship and psychologically "joining" with the child and their family are important first steps in obtaining trust. Proper introductions and spending a few minutes in nonthreatening social conversation will put the child and his or her caretaker at ease.

Prepare for the interview with the child by initially talking with their guardian about the nature and extent of suspected abuse. The interview should include the following (Finkelhor, 1993):

A past medical history

A medical-psychological review of systems for abuse-related problems

A family history

A social history

A developmental history

Do not discuss the abuse allegations with the others while the child is listening or in the same room.

When interviewing the child, set up the environment so that the child feels comfortable. Interview the child without the accompanying adult present, if at all possible. Be positive and supportive. Establish rapport. Ask about school, pets, friends, hobbies, or interests. Ask about living arrangements and who is in the family. Inquire why the child thinks they are at the doctor. For example, ask, "Did your mommy tell you why she wanted you to come to the clinic today to see me?"

Ask open-ended questions. "Why are you here today?" "Has any one ever touched you in a way that makes you feel uncomfortable?" "Has anybody ever hurt you or made you feel bad?" "What is the worst thing that ever happened to you?" If a child tells you they have been touched or hurt, they can often point to the parts of the body that were touched, even if they cannot name those parts. Some children will answer only "yes-no" questions, in which case the interviewer should be careful to avoid asking leading questions or questions that suggest an answer.

Ask about pain, bleeding, events preceding and following the abuse episodes, who else was there, what the abuser said, what people were wearing, and where the abuse occurred. Pin down the identity of the abuser if you can do it in a nonleading way. Ask about threats. Reassure the child that he or she is safe.

Older children will often give the examiner specific, clear descriptions of sexual abuse. Younger children will be harder to interview and understand. Experienced interviewers and play therapists have developed ways to talk with very young children about abuse. These skills are not often part of medical practice (Levitt, 1992).

Use toys, crayons, markers, and visual aids if you are skilled in these techniques and make time for more extensive interviewing. Although many children who have been abused will exhibit sexual themes in their drawings, these findings are not specific and should be interpreted with caution (Hibbard, Roghmann, & Hoekelman, 1987). Anatomically detailed dolls can be a useful adjunct to interviewing. The skillful use of the dolls requires training and sensitivity, for which specific protocols have been developed (White, Strom, Santilli, & Halpin, 1986). However, examiners without training and experience in the use of dolls may not find it particularly helpful. When a child demonstrates sexual acts with the dolls, it may be suggestive of a history of abuse, but it is not diagnostic. The best use of the dolls is for the child to confirm verbal reports of abuse by demonstrating what happened to them.

Children's responses to interviews about abuse depend on several factors (Giardino, Finkel, Giardino, Seidl, & Ludwig, 1992; Steward, Bussey, Goodman, & Saywitz, 1993), including the following:

1. Their level of cognitive development and their ability to understand abstractions such as time, dates, and their motives;

2. Their emotional development, including their level of dependence on the family and ability to view themselves within the context of relationships, and use of emotional defenses, such as repression and denial;

3. Their behavioral development, including their awareness of limits and expectations, attention span, identity, and independence;

4. The characteristics of the sexual abuse, their relationship to the offender, the duration and nature of the offenses, threats used, and the degree of violence or trauma the children experienced; and

5. The response of people in the children's environment to the disclosure. Children will be afraid to report because of possible repudiation and rejection by their families. Supportive families will facilitate disclosure.

Whether or not to record the interview on audio or video tape is debatable (Meyers, 1993). Some experienced clinicians favor this process, whereas others do not. It is wise to consult social service agencies, police, and prosecutors in your jurisdiction before committing to this process.

After an interview, close by telling the child that they did the right thing by talking about the abuse. Acknowledge how difficult it was for them. Be supportive and accepting. After the physical examination, tell the child that they are healthy and normal. Older children will often appreciate being reassured that they look just like other kids their age and can grow up and get married and have babies just like everybody else, if they want to. Give the child a chance to ask questions. Explain the findings to the child's caretaker.

Skillful medical interviewing requires time, training, patience, and practice. Physicians who do not have all four should defer interviewing in sexual abuse cases to other professionals.

STUDY QUESTIONS

4. What are some signs and symptoms of child sexual abuse?

5. What principles should be followed when interviewing children in a medical setting for suspected child sexual abuse?

6. What are some of the factors that influence children's responses to interviews about abuse?

7. What are some ways of alleviating stress for the child during physical examination?

Physical Examination
of Sexually Abused Children

The medical practitioner has a unique role in the evaluation of sexually abused children by gathering evidence not available to others during a general physical examination to assess their health status, as well as during a genital and anal examination. The examination should document any physical abuse or neglect, assess growth and development, and document injuries to the genitalia or anus.

Before examining the child, obtain height, weight, and head circumference measurements and plot these on standard growth charts. As part of the examination, bitemarks and other cutaneous injuries are documented (Tipton, 1989; Wagner, 1986). Photographs of marks should include a size standard and color bar. If photography is unavailable, careful drawings and descriptions of marks should be done. A general screening physical examination may reveal occult health problems or untreated chronic illness.

Carefully preparing the child for genital and anal examinations can decrease the amount of anxiety and stress the child experiences because of the examination (American Academy of Pediatrics Committee on Child Abuse and Neglect, 1991). Before the exam, have the child choose who will be present (e.g., mother, social worker, etc.). Giving the child a choice over details, such as the color of gown and drape used, can provide them with a sense of control. All procedures and equipment can be explained in detail, including the colposcope. The child will be less fearful if they have a chance to look through the colposcope and have the light shined on the skin of the hand to demonstrate how painless it is.

Distracting the child during the exam can also help to alleviate their stress. Singing, counting, reciting nursery rhymes, identifying objects in a book or poster, or talking about pleasant experiences will encourage the child to relax. The liberal use of drapes to protect the child's sense of modesty can also help.

Female children can be examined in the supine, frog-leg position, knee-chest position, or both (Herman-Giddens & Frothingham, 1987). Usually, children do not like to assume knee-chest position, because of discomfort or lack of a sense of control, but it is an excellent way to elucidate introital anatomy. Most examiners would recommend using knee-chest position whenever the introitus appears abnormal or questionable in frog-leg position.

In frog-leg position, the labia are pulled laterally and down to expose the internal structures of the introitus. Gentle traction by the examiner on the labia majora (i.e., pulling them toward the examiner and slightly laterally) can also be helpful. In knee-chest position, the labia are separated and pulled up and laterally toward the buttocks. The hymen may appear different when examined in knee-chest instead of frog-leg position. The vertical transhymenal diameter is likely to appear larger in knee-chest position, and the transverse horizontal hymenal diameter is likely to appear larger when using labial traction in the supine position (McCann, Voris, Simon, & Wells, 1990).

If the child has a redundant hymen, the flaps of the hymen can be separated to look for tears or lesions. Older children may tolerate separation of the hymeneal flaps with a moistened cotton swab. For younger children, this might be perceived as painful. Rinsing the genitalia with sterile saline will usually allow the hymen to be adequately examined and is generally well accepted by the child.

Prepubertal girls do not need to be examined internally (above the level of the hymen) unless there is upper tract bleeding, presence of a vaginal foreign body, or other vaginal pathology present (Botash, 1994). If an internal, upper tract examination is indicated, most children will tolerate the procedure better if sedated or anesthetized. Some abused girls cannot tolerate even an external examination. In these cases, the examiner should decide if the need for an examination is worth the risk of sedation or anesthesia (Harari & Netzer, 1994). Often, if the child can get to know the examiner by returning to the clinic for more visits, trust can be established and the child can be examined while awake. It is important for the examiner to realize the potential for "retraumatizing" the child with a genital exam and to guard against it by being sensitive to the child's needs.

A rectal-abdominal bimanual palpation of pelvic organs can be done on prepubertal girls, if the examination of the uterus is indicated. This is less uncomfortable than a vaginal-abdominal bimanual exam. A pelvic ultrasound can also be used to avoid the need for a bimanual exam in a prepubertal child.

Adolescent girls who have had sexual intercourse need to have a vaginal speculum examination and a bimanual examination of pelvic organs (Emans, 1988). They require Papanicolaou smears and cervical cultures. Often, an examination resulting from an abuse disclosure will be their first pelvic examination. The examiner should be extremely sensitive to the potential emotional trauma caused by the abuse. Exams should be carefully explained and gently executed.

Normal Physical Findings in Anal and Genital Examinations. The work of McCann and colleagues (McCann, Voris, Simon, & Wells, 1989; McCann et al., 1990), Pokorny (1987; Pokorny & Kozinetz, 1988), and Berenson (1993a, 1993b; Berenson, Heger, Hayes, Bailey, & Emans, 1992) has provided us with ground-breaking information on the anal and genital anatomy of normal prepubertal children. A review of their work is essential for anyone working in the field of child abuse. One cannot appreciate *abnormal* anatomy unless one recognizes normal anatomy.

Appendix 1 lists basic anatomical terminology of prepubertal female genitalia. The terms included have been adopted by the American Professional Society on the Abuse of Children in their *Guidelines on Medical Terminology.*

The size of the hymeneal opening will differ with the examination position and technique (McCann, Voris, et al., 1990), the age of the child, and the degree of relaxation of the child. Although children with absent or torn hymens will have enlarged hymeneal openings, there is also a wide range of normal sizes in children with intact, undamaged hymens. It is best to evaluate the hymeneal diameter in relation to other signs of fresh or healed trauma in the introitus, rather than considering it as a single measurement unrelated to other findings.

Normal Anatomic Variants, Pathologic Conditions, and Conditions Resulting From Trauma Not Related to Sexual Abuse That Are Commonly Confused With Sexual Abuse. A variety of normal and pathological conditions can mimic trauma in prepubertal children (Bays & Jenny, 1990). This points out the importance of a history of sexual abuse from the child when making the diagnosis. Nonetheless, when trauma is evident, it cannot be ignored, even if the child denies any abuse. Thus, recognition of conditions mimicking abuse is necessary for examiners.

The two most common conditions confused with abuse are lichen sclerosis (Jenny, Kirby, & Fuquay, 1989) and *Streptococcus pyogenes* infections of the genitalia and anus. Lichen sclerosis is a skin disease causing thinning and atrophy of perianal and perigenital skin. The skin bleeds and bruises with the slightest amount of pressure and appears to have been traumatized. B-hemolytic streptococcal infections can cause severe pain and erythema of the anus or genitals. Both of these conditions are easy to recognize if the examiner keeps them in mind when examining children for sexual abuse trauma.

Common Physical Findings of the Genitalia and Anus Related to Sexual Abuse Trauma. Sexual abuse trauma can be acute, subacute (healing), or chronic (healed). In many documented cases of abuse, the physical examination of the child has been found to be normal (Muram, 1989b). A normal physical examination does not rule out sexual abuse. Many types of abuse do not leave any permanent physical scars. Some trauma will heal completely (McCann, Voris, & Simon, 1989). In addition, children continue to grow and develop after abuse occurs, so often, signs of past abuse are masked by the changes that occur with sexual development (Finkel, 1989).

Certain types of physical findings are considered diagnostic of penetrating injury to the vagina, including lack of hymenal tissue, hymeneal lacerations, notching in the posterior half of the hymen, and scars (Emans, Woods, Flagg, & Freeman, 1987; Kerns, Ritter, & Thomas, 1992).

Scars in the fossa navicularis must be distinguished from the normal "white areas" found in normal children in that region (McCann, Wells, et al., 1990). Splits of posterior labial fusions can look like posterior fourchette tears (McCann, Voris, & Simon, 1988). Median raphe and fusion abnormalities on the perineal body can mimic perineal body scars (Adams & Horton, 1989).

Most trauma to the genitals of boys is obvious on physical examination, including erythema, swelling, lacerations, ligature injuries, and bitemarks. Boys are more likely to suffer anal injuries during abuse, rather than genital injuries (De Jong, Emmett, & Hervada, 1982).

Penetrating anal trauma can cause anal tears, circumferential fissures, triangular abrasions, edema, and inflammation. Chronic penetration can lead to loss of anal tone or scarring of the muscle layer, causing asymmetry of the anus. Even after acute, violent trauma causing anal tears, children can heal completely without residual scarring (Muram, 1989a).

STUDY QUESTIONS

8. Describe the techniques for physical examination of the genitalia and anus.

9. When are internal speculum and bimanual examinations indicated?

10. Why is it essential to know how to recognize normal genital and anal findings?

11. What are the normal anatomic variants, pathologic conditions, and conditions resulting from trauma not related to sexual abuse that are commonly confused with sexual abuse?

12. Describe the common physical findings of the genitalia and anus related to acute, subacute, and healed sexual abuse trauma.

13. What are the changes in sexual abuse trauma that may occur with healing over time?

USE OF THE PHOTOCOLPOSCOPE

There are both advantages and disadvantages in using the photocolposcope in cases of sexual abuse. Photocolposcopy has been used extensively to evaluate child sexual abuse (McCann, 1990). Using the colposcope provides several important advantages (Adams, Phillips, & Ahmad, 1990). The magnification and excellent light source allow for detailed examination of the genitals and anus. Photography of colposcopic exams allows for confirmation of examination findings and increases the accuracy and consistency of diagnosis. It also allows for second opinions to be obtained without requiring reexamination of the child. Using photography decreases the time required for exams, because examiners can get another look at findings after the photos are developed.

The entire field of genital and anal pathology after abuse has developed because of photocolposcopy. Researchers have been able to share clinical experience and reach a consensus about the meaning of physical findings. Colposcopic photos are also invaluable for teaching. Finally, colposcopic photos can be presented effectively in court as corroborative evidence of sexual assault or abuse.

The major disadvantage of colposcopy is the cost. Using the photocolposcope raises the cost of a medical examination substantially. Also, some lawyers argue that using the colposcope is the "standard of care," which discredits examiners who do not have access to colposcopes. However, Muram and Elias (1989) did not show a substantial difference in lesions noted using the colposcope as opposed to those examined with the unaided eye.

DOCUMENTING THE MEDICAL
CHART IN SEXUAL ABUSE CASES

A well-prepared chart is necessary for medical practitioners to preserve evidence and factual information in sexual abuse cases. Information on the child's affect, language skills, and reaction to the examination is important. Direct quotes from the child can be used to substantiate abuse allegations. When a case is eventually heard in court months or years after the child was seen, a detailed medical chart can help the practitioner be a more effective witness.

S T U D Y   Q U E S T I O N

14. What are the advantages of using the photocolposcope and other methods of documentation in the examination? What are the disadvantages?

References

Adams, J. A., & Horton, M. (1989). Is it sexual abuse? Confusion caused by a congenital anomaly of the genitalia. *Clinical Pediatrics (Philadelphia), 28,* 146-148.

Adams, J. A., Phillips, P., & Ahmad, M. (1990). The usefulness of colposcopic photographs in the evaluation of suspected child sexual abuse. *Adolescent Pediatrics and Gynecology, 3,* 75-82.

American Academy of Pediatrics Committee on Child Abuse and Neglect. (1991). Guidelines for the evaluation of sexual abuse of children. *Pediatrics, 87,* 254-259.

Bays, J., & Jenny, C. (1990). Genital and anal conditions confused with child sexual abuse trauma. *American Journal of Diseases of Children, 144,* 1319-1322.

Berenson, A. B. (1993a). Appearance of the hymen at birth and one year of age: A longitudinal study. *Pediatrics, 91,* 820-825.

Berenson, A. B. (1993b). Perianal findings in infants 18 months of age or younger. *Pediatrics, 91,* 838-840.

Berenson, A. B., Heger, A. H., Hayes, J. M., Bailey, R. K., & Emans, S. J. (1992). Appearance of the hymen in prepubertal girls. *Pediatrics, 89,* 387-394.

Berkowitz, C. D. (1987). Sexual abuse of children and adolescents. *Advances in Pediatrics, 34,* 275-312.

Botash, A. S. (1994). What the office-based pediatricians need to know about child sexual abuse. *Contemporary Pediatrics, 11,* 83-84, 87, 91-94, 97-98, 100.

De Jong, A. R., Emmett, G. A., & Hervada, A. A. (1982). Epidemiologic factors in sexual abuse of boys. *American Journal of Diseases of Children, 136,* 990-993.

Emans, S. J. (1988). Evaluation of sexually abused child and adolescent. *Adolescent and Pediatric Gynecology, 1,* 157-163.

Emans, S. J., Woods, E. R., Flagg, N. T., & Freeman, A. (1987). Genital findings in sexually abused, symptomatic, and asymptomatic girls. *Pediatrics, 79,* 778-785.

Finkel, M. A. (1989). Anogenital trauma in sexually abused children. *Pediatrics, 84,* 317-322.

Finkelhor, D. (1993). Epidemiological factors in the clinical identification of child sexual abuse. *Child Abuse & Neglect, 17,* 67-70.

Friedrich, W. N., Grambsch, P., Broughton, D., Kuiper, J., & Beilke, R. L. (1991). Normative sexual behavior in children. *Pediatrics, 88*(3), 456-464.

Gallagher, P. (1993). Medical examination of children thought to have been sexually abused. *Medical Science Law, 33,* 203-206.

Giardino, A. P., Finkel, M. A., Giardino, E. R., Seidl, T., & Ludwig, S. (1992). *A practical guide to the evaluation of sexual abuse in the prepubertal child* (pp. 19-28). Newbury Park, CA: Sage.

Harari, M., & Netzer, D. (1994). Genital examination under ketamine sedation in cases of suspected sexual abuse. *Archives of Diseases in Childhood, 70,* 197-199.

Herman-Giddens, M. E., & Frothingham, T. E. (1987). Prepubertal female genitalia: Examination for evidence of sexual abuse. *Pediatrics, 80,* 203-208.

Hibbard, R. A., Roghmann, K., & Hoekelman, R. A. (1987). Genitalia in children's drawings: An association with sexual abuse. *Pediatrics, 79,* 129-137.

Hunter, R. S., Kilstrom, N., & Loda, F. (1985). Sexually abused children: Identifying masked presentations in a medical setting. *Child Abuse & Neglect, 9,* 17-25.

Jenny, C., Kirby, P., & Fuquay, D. (1989). Genital lichen sclerosis mistaken for child sexual abuse. *Pediatrics, 83,* 597-599.

Jones, D. P. H., & McQuiston, M. (1984). Interviewing the sexually abused child, II: Principles and practice. In D. C. Bross (Ed.), *Multidisciplinary advocacy for mistreated children* (pp. 159-181). Denver, CO: National Association of Counsel for Children.

Kanda, M., Thomas, J. N., & Lloyd, D. W. (1985). The role of forensic evidence in the evaluation of child abuse and neglect. *American Journal of Forensic Medicine and Pathology, 6,* 7-15.

Kerns, D. L., Ritter, M. L., & Thomas, R. G. (1992). Concave hymenal variations in suspected child sexual abuse victims. *Pediatrics, 90,* 458-460.

Krugman, R. D. (1986). Recognition of sexual abuse in children. *Pediatrics in Review, 8*(1), 25-30.

Leventhal, J. M. (1988). Have there been changes in the epidemiology of sexual abuse of children during the 20th century? *Pediatrics, 82*(5), 766-773.

Levitt, C. J. (1992). The medical interview. In A. Heger & S. J. Emans (Eds.), *Evaluation of the sexually abused child: A medical textbook and photographic atlas* (pp. 31-38). New York: Oxford University Press.

MacFarlane, K., & Krebs, S. (1986). Techniques for interviewing and evidence gathering. In K. MacFarlane & J. Waterman (Eds.), *Sexual abuse of young children: Evaluation and treatment* (pp. 67-100). New York: Guilford.

McCann, J. (1990). Use of the colposcope in childhood sexual abuse examinations. *Pediatric Clinic, North America, 37,* 863-868.

McCann, J., Voris, J., & Simon, M. (1988). Labial adhesions and posterior fourchette injuries in childhood sexual abuse. *American Journal of Diseases of Children, 142,* 659-663.

McCann, J., Voris, J., & Simon, M. (1989). Genital injuries resulting from sexual abuse: A longitudinal study. *Pediatrics, 89,* 307-317.

McCann, J., Voris, J., Simon, M., & Wells, R. (1989). Perianal findings in prepubertal children selected for nonabuse: A descriptive study. *Child Abuse & Neglect, 13,* 179-193.

McCann, J., Voris, J., Simon, M., & Wells, R. (1990). Comparison of genital examination techniques in prepubertal girls. *Pediatrics, 85,* 182-187.

McCann, J., Wells, R., Simon, M., & Voris, J. (1990). Genital finding in prepubertal girls selected for nonabuse: A descriptive study. *Pediatrics, 86,* 428-439.

McLeer, S. V., Deblinger, E., Atkins, M. S., Foa, E. B., & Ralphe, D. L. (1988). Post-traumatic stress disorder in sexually abused children. *Journal of the American Academy of Child and Adolescent Psychiatry, 27,* 650-654.

Meyers, J. E. B. (1993). Investigative interviews of children: Should they be videotaped? *Notre Dame Journal of Law, Ethics, & Public Policy, 7,* 371-386.

Muram, D. (1989a). Anal and perianal abnormalities in prepubertal victims of sexual abuse. *American Journal of Obstetrics and Gynecology, 1619,* 278-281.

Muram, D. (1989b). Child sexual abuse: Relationship between sexual acts and genital findings. *Child Abuse & Neglect, 13,* 211-216.

Muram, D., & Elias, S. (1989). Child sexual abuse: Genital tract findings in prepubertal girls, II: Comparison of colposcopic and unaided examination. *American Journal of Obstetrics and Gynecology, 160,* 333-335.

National Center on Child Abuse and Neglect. (1981). *Study findings: National study of the incidence and severity of child abuse and neglect* (DHHS Publication No. OHDS 81-30325). Washington, DC: Government Printing Office.

Pokorny, S. F. (1987). Configuration of the prepubertal hymen. *American Journal of Obstetrics and Gynecology, 157,* 950-956.

Pokorny, S. F., & Kozinetz, C. A. (1988). Configuration and other anatomic details of the prepubertal hymen. *Adolescent and Pediatric Gynecology, 1,* 97-103.

Seidel, J. S., Elvik, S. L., Berkowitz, C. D., & Day, C. (1986). Presentation and evaluation of sexual misuse in the emergency department. *Pediatric Emergency Care, 24,* 157-164.

Smith, D. S., Losek, J. D., Glaeser, P. W., & Walsh-Kelly, C. (1988). Pediatric sexual abuse management in a sample of children's hospitals. *Pediatric Emergency Care, 4,* 177-179.

Steward, M. S., Bussey, K., Goodman, G. S., & Saywitz, K. J. (1993). Implications of developmental research for interviewing children. *Child Abuse & Neglect, 17,* 25-38.

Tipton, A. C. (1989). Child sexual abuse: Physical examination techniques and interpretation of findings. *Adolescent and Pediatric Gynecology, 2*(1), 10-25.

Wagner, G. N. (1986). Bitemark identification in child abuse cases. *Pediatric Dentistry, 8,* 96-100.

White, S., Strom, G. A., Santilli, G., & Halpin, B. M. (1986). Interviewing young sexual abuse victims with anatomically correct dolls. *Child Abuse & Neglect, 10,* 519-529.

Forensic Examination of the Sexually Assaulted Child

Basic References

Gaensslen, R. E. (1983). *Sourcebook in forensic serology, immunology, and biochemistry.* Washington, DC: National Institute of Justice, Government Printing Office.

This book contains a vast amount of information on forensic science and the identification of sex offenders based on material collected from victims and crime scenes. Although the book is over a decade old, no treatise can match it for comprehensive information. It is a helpful reference guide for people working with sexual assault victims.

Jenny, C. (1992). Forensic examination: The role of the physician as "medical detective." In A. H. Heger & S. J. Emans (Eds.), *Evaluation of the sexually abused child: A medical textbook and photographic atlas.* Boston: Oxford University Press.

This chapter gives an overview for clinicians on the methods and materials needed to conduct a competent sexual assault examination.

Kanda, M., Thomas, J. N., & Lloyd, D. W. (1985). The role of forensic evidence in child abuse and neglect. *American Journal of Forensic Medicine and Pathology, 6,* **7-15.**

The authors in this classic article outline the physician's role in rape examinations.

National Research Council Committee on DNA Technology in Forensic Science. (1992). *DNA technology in forensic science.* **Washington, DC: National Academy Press.**

Although it is not light reading and is not likely to be read cover to cover by nonscientists, this work contains a state-of-the-art description of the status of forensic DNA typing and serves as an excellent resource book.

Rapps, W. R. (1980). Scientific evidence in rape prosecution. *University of Missouri at Kansas City Law Review, 48,* **216-236.**

Although somewhat dated, this article is still an extremely useful review of forensic serology and biochemistry.

Discussion

CONDUCTING FORENSIC EXAMINATIONS

Collection, handling, and storage of forensic specimens to maintain a chain of custody of evidence is important so that evidence can be presented in courts of law. The samples collected from acutely sexually assaulted children must be protected from contamination, degradation, or tampering by storing it in locked cabinets, refrigerators, or freezers. Freezers that maintain constant temperatures below −10° C. are needed for optimal preservation of biological evidence, such as specimens for deoxyribonucleic acid (DNA) typing (Jenny, 1992).

Forensic examinations should be done according to a specific protocol (Kanda, Thomas, & Lloyd, 1985). In some jurisdictions, the protocol is provided by law enforcement. In other states, each hospital maintains its own protocol and storage materials. Protocols specify how to handle materials, including clothes or shoes worn by the victim, pubic hair and head hair, fingernail scrapings and clippings, and trace evidence, such as dirt or grass found on the victim's body. These are usually stored in paper bags, which are sealed and labeled.

Before examining the child, a Wood's lamp is used to scan any part of the body where semen might be found. Semen or other oily substances will fluoresce a blue-green to orange color, as will other substances, such as urine (Gabby et al., 1992). These areas can be swabbed with saline-moistened cotton swabs to recover genetic markers from the semen.

Before obtaining other forensic specimens or using a speculum, toluidine blue dye can be applied to the posterior fourchette to detect nucleated epithelial cells exposed by traumatic laceration of the skin. Superficial lacerations of the skin may not be visible without the use of the dye. McCauley, Gorman, and Guzinski (1986) found the use of toluidine dye to significantly increase the number of lacerations detected in sexually abused children.

Permanent smears to detect sperm should be taken from assaulted orifices (Gaensslen, 1983). These can be preserved as Papanicolaou smears or as air-dried smears. A saline wet mount should be done by the examiner to detect motile or nonmotile sperm. Saline-moistened swabs can also be used to swab body cavities for genetic markers of semen, although vaginal washes will yield better specimens for DNA typing (N. A. Buroker, personal communication, July 10, 1990). The washes will dilute other genetic markers, however. Any moistened swabs should be thoroughly air-dried before freezing. It is important to obtain more than one swab per body cavity so that evidence material can be saved for analysis by any legal defense.

Immediately after the physical examination, wet mounts obtained from the assaulted body cavities should be examined for motile and nonmotile sperm. The wet mount can be performed from obtained washings, or a separate swab can be placed in a small quantity of normal saline, kept at body temperature, and examined under a microscope. When the saline is maintained at body temperature, motility of sperm and microorganisms are more likely to be preserved (Judson & Ehret, 1994).

What happens to samples collected in a "rape kit" when they are processed in a forensic science laboratory? Swabs can be eluted to search for sperm. Swabs, washes, and clothing can be tested for acid phosphatase, which is found in high concentrations in semen (Findley, 1977; Sensabaugh, 1979).

Tests can also be done for semen-specific proteins. Examples include p30 protein and MHS-5 antigen (Graves, Sensabaugh, & Blake, 1985; Herr & Woodward, 1986).

Testing for heterogeneous proteins in saliva and semen, such as ABO blood group proteins (Daview, 1989), phosphoglucomutase (Price, Daview, & Wraxall, 1976), and peptidase A (Parkin, 1981), can rule in or rule out suspected perpetrators based on biochemical evidence. Hair found at the crime scene or left on the patient's body can be compared with a suspect's hair and with controls obtained from the patient.

DNA typing offers a powerful new type of evidence (McCabe, 1992). DNA isolated from blood, semen, or other body tissues is analyzed for restriction fragment length polymorphisms. Considerable identifying information can be obtained that can be used to calculate the likelihood of tissue match with the alleged offender. DNA typing offers a more specific level of biochemical evidence. As the tests available to forensic scientists improve, the correct collection and preservation of evidence by physicians and nurses takes on new importance in the protection of victims.

LEGAL REQUIREMENTS
FOR CHART DOCUMENTATION

A medical record in a child sexual abuse case can become evidence presented in a court of law. Social service workers, police, prosecutors, and defense lawyers depend on these records in making decisions affecting the child and the accused perpetrator. The accuracy, completeness, and legibility of the record will enhance the efficiency and fairness of the criminal justice and child protection systems (Indest, 1989).

When recording a child's history of abuse, use direct quotes from the child. Most states have enacted exceptions to their "hearsay laws" that allow medical practitioners to present children's descriptions of abuse to juries. The accurate recording of disclosures of abuse can facilitate their presentation in court (Kermani, 1993). Medical practitioners should also record the questions they ask that evoke the answer from the child.

Colposcopic or macroscopic photographs can be helpful in documenting genital, anal, and other injuries (McCann, 1990; Ricci, 1988). Practitioners who regularly evaluate abused children should have excellent photographic equipment available. Otherwise, careful anatomic drawings in the chart should demonstrate lesions. Videocolposcopy is being used in some centers to record anal and genital examinations. The technology is relatively expensive and time-consuming but is an excellent teaching tool and provides instant feedback of the documentation. Whether or not this tool yields more accurate examination documentation remains to be seen.

STUDY QUESTIONS

1. Why is the collection, handling, and storage of forensic specimens so important in cases of child sexual abuse?

2. Describe the principles of forensic examination and specimen collection after acute sexual assault.

3. What are the basic scientific principles underlying the application of forensic microscopy, serology, and biochemistry, in sexual assault cases?

4. What are the legal requirements for chart documentation in child sexual abuse cases?

References

Daview, A. (1989). Scientific examination in sexual assault. *Medical Law, 8,* 331-335.

Findley, T. P. (1977). Quantitation of vaginal acid phosphatase and its relationship to time of coitus. *American Journal of Clinical Pathology, 68,* 238-242.

Gabby, T., Winkleby, M. A., Boyce, W. T., Fisher, D. L., Lancaster, A., & Sensabaugh, G. F. (1992). Sexual abuse of children: The detection of semen on skin. *American Journal of Diseases of Children, 146,* 700-703.

Gaensslen, R. E. (1983). Identification of semen and vaginal secretions. In R. E. Gaensslen (Ed.), *Sourcebook in forensic serology, immunology, and biochemistry* (pp. 149-181). Washington, DC: National Institute of Justice, Government Printing Office.

Graves, H. C., Sensabaugh, G. F., & Blake, E. T. (1985). Postcoital detection of a male-specific semen protein by ELISA: Application to rape investigation. *New England Journal of Medicine, 312,* 338-343.

Herr, J. C., & Woodward, M. P. (1986). An enzyme-linked immunosorbent assay (ELISA) for human semen identification based on a biotinylated monoclonal antibody to a seminal vesicle-specific antigen. *Journal of Forensic Science, 32,* 346-356.

Indest, G. F. III. (1989). Medico-legal issues in detecting and proving the sexual abuse of children. *Journal of Sex and Marital Therapy, 15,* 141-160.

Jenny, C. (1992). Forensic examination: The role of the physician as "medical detective." In A. H. Heger & S. J. Emans (Eds.), *Evaluation of the sexually abused child: A medical textbook and photographic atlas.* Boston: Oxford University Press.

Judson, F. N., & Ehret, J. (1994). Laboratory diagnosis of sexually transmitted infections. *Pediatric Annals, 23,* 361-369.

Kanda, M., Thomas, J. N., & Lloyd, D. W. (1985). The role of forensic evidence in child abuse and neglect. *American Journal of Forensic Medicine and Pathology, 6,* 7-15.

Kermani, E. J. (1993). Child sexual abuse revisited by the U.S. Supreme Court. *Journal of the American Academy of Child and Adolescent Psychiatry, 32,* 971-974.

McCabe, E. R. (1992). Applications of DNA fingerprinting in pediatric practice. *Journal of Pediatrics, 120,* 499-509.

McCann, J. (1990). Use of the colposcope in childhood sexual abuse examinations. *Pediatric Clinic, North America, 37,* 863-880.

McCauley, J., Gorman, R. L., & Guzinski, G. (1986). Toluidine blue in the detection of perineal lacerations in pediatric and adolescent sexual abuse victims. *Pediatrics, 78,* 1039-1043.

Parkin, B. (1981). The evidential value of peptidase A as a semen typing system. *Journal of Forensic Science, 26,* 398-404.

Price, C. J., Daview, A., & Wraxall, B. G. (1976). The typing of phosphoglucomutase in vaginal material and semen. *Journal of the Forensic Science Society, 16,* 29-42.

Ricci, L. R. (1988). Medical forensic photography of the sexually abused child. *Child Abuse & Neglect, 12,* 305-310.

Sensabaugh, G. F. (1979). The quantitative acid phosphatase test. *Journal of Forensic Science, 24,* 346-365.

Sexually Transmitted Diseases in Children

Basic References

Centers for Disease Control and Prevention. (1993). 1993 sexually transmitted diseases treatment guidelines. *Morbidity and Mortality Weekly, 42*(No. RR-14), 1-102.

This edition of *Morbidity and Mortality Weekly* provides the most recent treatment guidelines from the Centers for Disease Control and Prevention.

Holmes, K. K., Mårdh, P. A., Sparling, P. F., Wiesner, P. J., Cates, W. Jr., Lemon, S. M., & Stamm, W. E. (1990). *Sexually transmitted diseases* (2nd ed.). New York: McGraw-Hill.

This book, the most complete and comprehensive in the field, is an important reference for professionals working with children and sexually transmitted diseases (STD).

Jenny, C. (Ed.). (1994). Sexually transmitted diseases. *Pediatric Annals, 23,* 329-374.

This issue of Pediatric Annals reviews new information on child abuse and STD.

Discussion

NONVENEREAL PATHOGENS AND CONDITIONS

Most cases of vaginitis, vulvitis, and anal infections in children are not caused by STD pathogens but by common nonvenereal pathogens and conditions. Poor hygiene and pinworms (*Enterobius vermicularis*) are the most common culprits causing genital and anal inflammation, pain, itching, or all three (Pierce & Hart, 1992). Vaginal foreign bodies can also cause vaginal discharge and bleeding (Paradise & Willis, 1985). Absorbant polyacrylate cross-linked polymers can leak from disposable diapers and can be confused with vaginal discharge (Goldweber, 1994).

Microbiological studies of vulvovaginitis in children have shown two categories of pathogens to be commonly represented: upper respiratory pathogens and gram-negative enteric organisms (Paradise, Campos, Friedman, & Frishmuth, 1982; Wald, 1984). Specifically, *Streptococcus pyogenes, Streptococcus pneumoniae, Neisseria meningitides, Moraxella catarrhalis,* and *Haemophilus influenzae* are respiratory pathogens that can infect the immature vagina. Of the gram negatives, *Shigella* and *Yersinia* species can cause vaginitis (Watkins & Quan, 1984). *Candida* infections, however, are not likely to cause vaginitis in girls.

SEXUALLY TRANSMITTED PATHOGENS

*Epidemiology, Modes of
Transmission, and Legal Implications*

Sexually transmitted pathogens in children can indicate abusive contact, but in some cases, the epidemiology may be different from those in adults (Ingram et al., 1992). The American Academy of Pediatrics (1991) has issued guidelines for STD as related to the need to report suspected abuse. In their recommendations, a positive culture for gonorrhea or a positive syphilis serology (not congenital) is a definite indication of abuse and requires reporting. Other STD are probable indicators of abuse and also require reporting. Discussions of individual organisms follow.

Syphilis. When children acquire syphilis after birth, 95% of infections are likely to be due to sexual abuse (Ginsberg, 1983). Intimate contact with infected lesions is usually required for the transmission of the diseases (Neinstein, Goldenring, & Carpenter, 1984; Rawstron, Bromberg, & Hammerschlag, 1993).

Gonorrhea. After the first year of life, gonorrhea in children is unlikely to be due to any mode of infection other than sexual abuse (Branch & Paxton, 1965). Ingram (1989) recommends that any gonococcal infection in children, whereby the source of infection is not identified, should be categorized as "gonococcal infection, how acquired unknown," rather than as an infection due to environmental contamination or casual contact. The likelihood of the infection being caused by other than sexual abuse is low.

Chlamydia trachomatis. This is commonly transmitted from mother to child through the birth process (Alexander & Harrison, 1983). The infant's vagina and rectum can be infected, as well as the oropharynx and conjunctiva (Schacter et al., 1979). If untreated, perinatally acquired infections can persist for many months. One study showed persistence of infection for 28.5 months (Bell et al., 1992). Studies have clearly shown, however, that *Chlamydia trachomatis* is more commonly found in sexually abused children than in nonabused children (Hammerschlag et al., 1984; Ingram et al., 1984).

Condylomata Acuminata (Human Papilloma Virus, or HPV). Genital and anal warts in children have been linked to sexual contact (Gutman, Herman-Giddens, & Phelps, 1993). The likelihood that HPV infections are transmitted by nonsexual contact is debatable. HPV infections have been known to be transmitted from mother to child during birth (Smith, Johnson, & Cripe, 1991), and the virus can also remain latent in tissue for long periods of time (Ferenezy, Mitao, Nagai, Silverstein, & Crum, 1985). Whether or not infections in older children represent long-term carriage of the virus is unknown.

Herpes Virus Infections. Genital and anal herpes infections are frequently caused by sexual abuse of children (Kaplan, Fleisher, Paradise, & Friedman, 1984). Autoinoculation of a child's genitals from herpetic sores on or in the child's mouth has been reported (Nahmias, Dowdle, Naib, Josey, & Luce, 1968). Varicella virus infections (chicken pox) can also be confused with genital herpes. Type 2 herpes simplex infections are generally associated with genital infection and sexual contact. Type 1 herpes simplex infections are commonly transmitted nonsexually and cause oral infections in children. However, both types of herpes virus can cause either mouth or genital infections and can be sexually transmitted (Lafferty, Coombs, Benedetti, Critchlow, & Corey, 1987).

Trichomonas Vaginalis. Trichomonal infections in children are rare. They have been reported in sexually abused children (Jones, Yamauchi, & Lambert, 1985). Genital trichomoniasis requires contact between the child's genitals and infected secretions (Neinstein et al., 1984).

Diagnostic Tests

Diagnostic tests for sexually transmitted and associated microorganisms in children who have been sexually abused raise important issues with respect to evaluation. The Centers for Disease Control and Prevention (CDC) (1993) recommend the following be considered when deciding to test children for STD after alleged sexual assault or abuse:

1. Does the suspected offender have an STD or is the offender known to be at high risk for STD?
2. Does the child have signs or symptoms of STD?
3. Is there a high prevalence of STD in the community?

Female children with vaginitis are more likely to test positive for gonorrhea or *Chlamydia* than children evaluated for routine sexual abuse (Shapiro, Schubert, & Myers, 1993). A history of vaginal discharge should be considered in the decision whether or not to test abused children for STD.

When STD testing is done, the CDC recommends the following protocol (CDC, 1993).

Initial Evaluation and 2-Week Check (for acute assaults)

1. Cultures for *Neisseria gonorrhoeae* from the genitals, pharynx, and anus: Only standard culture systems should be used, and positive cultures should be confirmed with two tests that use different principles (biochemical tests, enzyme substrate tests, or serologic methods) (Whittington, Rice, Biddle, & Knapp, 1988).

2. Cultures for *Chlamydia trachomatis* from the vagina in girls and anus in both sexes: Nonculture tests should not be used (Hauger et al., 1988; Porder, Sanchez, Roblin, McHugh, & Hammerschlag, 1989).

3. Culture and wet mount of vaginal swabs for *Trichomonas vaginalis:* Wet mount should also be examined for bacterial vaginosis.

4. Collection of serum sample at the time of the initial visit: This should be saved for later testing if the child was assaulted less than 8 weeks before the visit.

Examination 12 Weeks After the Assault

Twelve weeks after the last sexual exposure, the child should receive serologic tests for syphilis, human immunodeficiency virus, and hepatitis B.

STUDY QUESTIONS

1. What are the common nonvenereal pathogens and conditions causing vulvitis, vaginitis, and anal infections in children?
2. What are the common sexually transmitted pathogens in children?
3. Describe the epidemiology, modes of transmission, and legal implications for each of the above pathogens in children.
4. When are diagnostic tests indicated for sexually transmitted and associated microorganisms in children?
5. What protocol does the CDC recommend for STD testing?

References

Alexander, E. R., & Harrison, H. R. (1983). Role of *Chlamydia trachomatis* in perinatal infection. *Reviews of Infectious Diseases, 5,* 713-719.

American Academy of Pediatrics Committee on Child Abuse and Neglect. (1991). Guidelines for the evaluation of sexual abuse of children. *Pediatrics, 87,* 254-260.

Bell, T. A., Stamm, W. E., Wang, S. P., Kuo, C. C., Holmes, K. K., & Grayston, T. G. (1992). Chronic *Chlamydia trachomatis* infections in infants. *Journal of American Medical Association, 267,* 400-402.

Branch, G., & Paxton, R. (1965). A study of gonococcal infections among infants and children. *Public Health Reports, 80*, 347-352.

Centers for Disease Control and Prevention. (1993). 1993 sexually transmitted diseases treatment guidelines. *Morbidity and Mortality Weekly, 42*(No. RR-14), 1-102.

Ferenezy, A., Mitao, M., Nagai, N., Silverstein, S. J., & Crum, C. P. (1985). Latent papillomavirus and recurring genital warts. *New England Journal of Medicine, 313*, 784-788.

Ginsberg, C. M. (1983). Acquired syphilis in prepubertal children. *Pediatric Infectious Disease Journal, 2*, 232-234.

Goldweber, R. T. (1994). "New" diapers and vaginal discharge (letter). *Pediatrics, 93*, 155.

Gutman, L. T., Herman-Giddens, M. E., & Phelps, W. C. (1993). Transmission of human genital papillomavirus disease: Comparison of data from adults and children. *Pediatrics, 91*, 31-38.

Hammerschlag, M. R., Doraiswamy, B., Alexander, E. R., Cox, P., Price, W., & Gleyzer, A. (1984). Are rectogenital chlamydial infections a marker of sexual abuse in children? *Pediatric Infectious Disease Journal, 3*, 100-104.

Hauger, S. B., Brown, J., Agre, F., Sahraie, F., Ortiz, R., & Ellner, P. (1988). Failure of direct fluorescent antibody staining to detect *Chlamydia trachomatis* from genital tract sites of prepubertal children at risk for sexual abuse. *Pediatric Infectious Disease Journal, 7*, 660-662.

Ingram, D. L. (1989). The gonococcus and the toilet seat revisited. *Pediatric Infectious Disease Journal, 8*, 191.

Ingram, D. L., Everett, V. D., Lyna, P. R., White, S. T., & Rockwell, L. A. (1992). Epidemiology of adult sexually transmitted disease agents in children being evaluated for sexual abuse. *Pediatric Infectious Disease Journal, 11*, 945-950.

Ingram, D. L., Runyan, D. K., Collins, A. D., White, S. T., Durfee, M. F., Pearson, A. W., & Occhiuti, A. R. (1984). Vaginal *Chlamydia trachomatis* infection in children with sexual contact. *Pediatric Infectious Disease Journal, 3*, 97-99.

Jones, J. G., Yamauchi, T., & Lambert, B. (1985). *Trichomonas vaginalis* infestation in sexually abused girls. *American Journal of Diseases of Children, 139*, 846-847.

Kaplan, K. M., Fleisher, G. R., Paradise, J. E., & Friedman, H. N. (1984). Social relevance of genital herpes simplex in children. *American Journal of Diseases of Children, 138*, 872-874.

Lafferty, W. E., Coombs, R. W., Benedetti, J., Critchlow, C., & Corey, L. (1987). Recurrences after oral and genital herpes simplex virus infection: Influence of site of infection and viral type. *New England Journal of Medicine, 316*, 1444-1449.

Nahmias, A. J., Dowdle, W. R., Naib, Z. M., Josey, W. E., & Luce, C. F. (1968). Genital infection with *Herpesvirus hominis* types 1 and 2 in children. *Pediatrics, 42*, 659-666.

Neinstein, L. S., Goldenring, J., & Carpenter, S. (1984). Nonsexual transmission of sexually transmitted diseases: An infrequent occurrence. *Pediatrics, 74,* 67-76.

Paradise, J. E., Campos, J. M., Friedman, H. M., & Frishmuth, G. (1982). Vulvovaginitis in premenarcheal girls: Clinical features and diagnostic evaluation. *Pediatrics, 70,* 193-198.

Paradise, J. E., & Willis, E. D. (1985). Probability of vaginal foreign body in girls with genital complaints. *American Journal of Diseases of Children, 139,* 472-476.

Pierce, A. M., & Hart, C. A. (1992). Vulvovaginitis: Causes and management. *Archives of Diseases in Childhood, 67,* 509-512.

Porder, K., Sanchez, N., Roblin, P. M., McHugh, M., & Hammerschlag, M. R. (1989). Lack of specificity of Chlamydiazyme for detection of vaginal chlamydial infection in prepubertal girls. *Pediatric Infectious Disease Journal, 8,* 358-360.

Rawstron, S. A., Bromberg, K., & Hammerschlag, M. R. (1993). STD in children: Syphilis and gonorrhea. *Genitourinary Medicine, 69,* 66-75.

Schacter, J., Grossman, M., Holt, J., Sweet, R., & Spector, S. (1979). Infection with *Chlamydia trachomatis:* Involvement of multiple anatomic sites in neonates. *Journal of Infectious Diseases, 139,* 232-234.

Shapiro, R. A., Schubert, C. J., & Myers, P. A. (1993). Vaginal discharge as an indicator of gonorrhea and *Chlamydia* infections in girls under 12 years old. *Pediatric Emergency Care, 9,* 341-345.

Smith, E. M., Johnson, S. R., & Cripe, T. P. (1991). Perinatal vertical transmission of human papillomavirus and subsequent development of respiratory tract papillomatosis. *Annals of Otology, Rhinology, and Laryngology, 100,* 479-483.

Wald, E. R. (1984). Gynecologic infections in the pediatric age group. *Pediatric Infectious Disease Journal, 3,* S10-S13.

Watkins, S., & Quan, L. (1984). Vulvovaginitis caused by *Yersinia enterocolitica. Pediatric Infectious Disease Journal, 3,* 444-445.

Whittington, W. L., Rice, R. J., Biddle, J. W., & Knapp, J. S. (1988). Incorrect identification of *Neisseria gonorrhoeae* from infants and children. *Pediatric Infectious Disease Journal, 7,* 3-10.

Appendix 1

Glossary of Medical Terms
in Physical Abuse

A

Abdomen The part of the trunk that lies between the thorax and the pelvis; belly

Abdominal Relating to the abdomen

Abdominal hematoma A hematoma (collection of blood) in the abdomen

Abrasion The removal of the epidermis of the skin or mucous membrane

Abscess A circumscribed collection of pus

Acromion A part of the scapula which forms a portion of the shoulder socket for the arm, and articulates with the clavicle (collar bone)

Adrenal glands Flattened, triangular bodies resting on the upper end of each kidney that secrete hormones

Affect Emotions, feelings, or moods expressed verbally or by one's physiognomy

Alkaline phosphatase An enzyme involved in bone metabolism and growth

Alopecia Abnormal hair loss; baldness

Alveolar margin The margin of the tooth sockets

Amylase A digestive enzyme produced by the pancreas and salivary glands; serum amylase levels are measured to detect injury and diseases of the pancreas

Anemia Decreased number of red blood cells, decreased hemoglobin, or decreased volume of red blood cells in the blood

Aneurysm A circumscribed dilation of an artery connected with the lumen of the artery

Anhidrosis Inability to perspire

Anoxic brain damage Brain damage caused by a decreased amount of oxygen in the tissues

Anterior In front of or in the front part of; ventral

Anterior chamber The space between the cornea and the iris of the eye filled with a watery fluid; the anterior chamber of the eye communicates with the posterior chamber through the pupil

Anterior longitudinal ligament of the spine A ligament connecting the anterior aspect of the vertebral bodies

Anterior-posterior diameter Distance from the front of the body to the back of the body

Anteroposterior (AP) views X-ray views of the body where the X-ray beam traverses the body from anterior to posterior, the patient's back against the film

Aorta The main trunk of the systemic arterial system, arising from the base of the left ventricle of the heart

Apgar score Evaluation of a newborn infant's physical status by assigning numerical values to heart rate, respiratory effort, muscle tone, reflex irritability, and skin color

Aplastic anemia Anemia caused by a severe decrease in the number of red blood cells and the amount of hemoglobin produced

Apnea To be without breath or respiration; inability to get a breath

Aponeurosis A fibrous sheet or expanded tendon attached to flat muscles

Arterial Relating to arteries

Arteriovenous malformation An abnormal connection between an artery and a vein

Aspiration The inspiratory sucking into the airways of fluid or foreign bodies

Asymmetrical Not symmetrical; denoting a lack of symmetry between two or more like parts

Asymptomatic Without symptoms, or producing no symptoms

Atrial Relating to the atrium (see *Atrium*)

Atrium The upper chamber of each half of the heart

Atrophy A wasting away of tissues, organs, or the whole body

Avulsion A tearing away

Axial skeleton The central part of the skeleton, including the skull and trunk, excluding the extremities

Axon The conducting portion of a nerve fiber

Axonal Relating to axons (see *Axon*)

B

Bilateral Relating to or having two sides

Bleeding time A laboratory test measuring how long a person bleeds when injured before clotting occurs; the bleeding time measures platelet/vessel interaction

Blood count Measurement of the numbers of formed elements in blood per volume unit

Blood dyscrasia Diseased state of the blood with abnormal cellular elements

Blunt Forward; direct

Blunt trauma Trauma caused by a blunt (non-penetrating) force

Bone scan A recording of the distribution of radioactive substances in the body after injection of radioisotopes into the bloodstream (also referred to as a scintigram)

Bruise A contusion producing a hematoma without rupture of the skin

C

Caffey's syndrome Infantile cortical hyperostosis; a benign, self-limited disease causing swelling of the bones

Callus The hard, bonelike substance that forms around and between the ends of bone fractures

Canthus Corner of the eye

Cardiac resuscitation Restoring heart function after cardiac arrest

Cardiomyopathy Disease of the myocardium (heart muscle)

Cataract A loss of transparency of the crystalline lens of the eye

Cephalohematoma A collection of blood under the pericranium (the fibrous membrane covering the skull)

Cerebral Relating to the cerebrum (see *Cerebrum*)

Cerebral palsy Paralysis resulting from brain injury

Cerebrospinal fluid The fluid circulating around the brain and spinal cord, also filling the ventricles inside the brain

Cerebrum The brain, including all parts except the pons, the medulla, and the cerebellum

Cervicofacial Relating to the neck and face

Chondrocyte Cartilage cell

Chylothorax An accumulation of milky, lymphatic fluid (chyle) in the thorax

Circulatory collapse Severe shock; failure of the circulatory system

Clavicle Collarbone

Clotting disorders Diseases that affect the blood clotting mechanism by clotting too much, too little, or not at all

Clotting studies Measurements of the blood's ability to clot

Coagulation disorders Clotting disorders

Coagulopathies Clotting disorders

Coat's disease Exudative retinitis with spontaneous retinal detachment

Columella The lower margin of the nasal septum (see *Nasal septum*)

Coma Unconsciousness; reduced mental alertness

Compliance The measure of the ease with which a structure may be deformed or expanded

Compression fracture An impaction of a bone caused by a force applied parallel to the long axis of the bone

Computerized tomography A diagnostic radiologic technique whereby a narrow, fan-shaped x-ray beam is passed through the patient; the amount of transmitted radiation is measured and analyzed, producing a computer-generated image of the internal structures of the body (CT)

Conduction system The structures conducting electrical impulses through the heart

Congenital Existing at birth

Conjunctiva The mucous membrane covering the anterior surface of the eyeball; the "whites of the eyes"

Consumption of coagulation factors The using up of factors needed for blood clotting, often caused by diffuse coagulation in the bloodstream or in tissues

Contusion A bruise

Coracoid process A process of the scapula (shoulder blade)

Cornea A transparent membrane forming the anterior outer coat of the eyeball

Cortical injury Damage to the cortex of the brain

CT Abbreviation for computerized tomography

Cyanocarylate adhesives Super glue

Cyanosis Bluish discoloration of the skin or mucous membranes due to lack of oxygen

Cyst A sac containing an abnormal accumulation of gas, fluid, or semisolid material

Cystic Relating to a cyst; also, relating to the bladder or gallbladder

D

Debilitating Causing weakness

Decelerate To slow down

Deceleration forces Forces causing injury to the body when the body slows and absorbs the force

Defibrillation The reversal of fibrillation of the cardiac muscle by applying an electric shock to the chest

Delirium A condition of extreme mental, and usually motor, excitement marked by confused and rapid unconnected ideas, often associated with hallucinations

Dental Relating to the teeth

Dentinogenesis imperfecta A hereditary condition causing the formation of defective dentin, resulting in easily fracturable, deformed teeth

Dermal Relating to the dermis (see *Dermis*)

Dermis The deep, connective tissue layer of the skin

Developmental quotients A measure of a child's level of development, comparing the level of development attained by the child with standardized developmental levels for that age

Diabetes mellitus A metabolic disease causing sugar to be excreted in the urine

Diaphysis The shaft or middle portion of a long bone

Diastatic Wide, separated

Differential diagnosis The list of all possible conditions considered in the diagnosis of a particular illness

Diffuse intravascular coagulation Clotting throughout the blood vessels, often consuming blood components necessary for coagulation, causing abnormal bleeding to result

Digit Finger or toe

Dislocation Disarrangement of the normal anatomic relationships of bones forming a joint

Disseminated intravascular coagulation See *Diffuse intravascular coagulation*

Duodenum The first division of the small intestine, about eleven inches or twelve finger-breadths (hence the name) in length, extending from the pylorus to the junction with the jejunum at the level of the first or second lumbar vertebra on the left side

Dural Relating to the dura mater (see *Dura mater*)

Dura mater A tough, fibrous envelope forming the outer envelope of the brain

Dysplasia Abnormal tissue development

Dysraphism Defective fusion of parts that usually come together (particularly the spine)

E

Ecchymosis A purplish patch caused by bleeding into the skin

Edema A perceptible accumulation of excessive fluid in the tissues

Engorgement Distention with fluid

Enzyme A protein secreted by the body cells that acts as a catalyst, inducing chemical changes in other substances, itself remaining apparently unchanged in the process

Epidemiology The science of epidemics and epidemic diseases

Epidermal Referring to the epidermis (see *Epidermis*)

Epidermis Cuticle; the outer epithelial portion of the skin

Epidural Outside the *dura mater* (see *Dura mater*)

Epiphyseal Relating to the epiphysis (see *Epiphysis*)

Epiphysis The end of the long bone that develops from a separate center of ossification from the shaft of the bone and is separated from the shaft of the long bone by a cartilaginous plate

Erythema Redness in the skin; inflammation

Erythema multiforme A skin disease, usually allergic in origin

Esophageal Relating to the esophagus (see *Esophagus*)

Esophagus The portion of the digestive canal between the pharynx and the stomach

Expressive language   The ability to express oneself through speaking or writing

Exsanguination   Depriving of blood; making exsanguine; often referring to the process of dying from a fatal hemorrhage

Exsanguine   Bloodless; anemic

Extension   Straightening a limb; diminishing the angle of a joint

External auditory canal   The passage leading inward from the external ear to the ear drum

Extrapleural   Outside the pleura (see *Pleura*)

F

Falx cerebri   A fold of dura mater in the longitudinal fissure between the two cerebral hemispheres

Fatal   Mortal; causing death

Femur   The large bone in the upper leg

Fetal   Relating to the fetus

Flexion   Bending a joint to approximate the parts it connects

Flexor creases   Creases in the tissues overlying a joint

Fontanelle   One of several membranous intervals at the angles of the cranial bones in the infant; in layman's terms, the "soft spot" on an infant's head

Fracture   A break in the bone or cartilage

Free fluid in the abdomen   Pathological collection of fluid within the abdominal cavity, not contained in organs or vessels (e.g., blood, spilled intestinal contents, lymph, or fluid resulting from inflammation)

Frenulum   A narrow reflection or fold of mucous membrane passing from a more fixed to a movable part, as from the gum to the deep surface of the lip, or from the floor of the mouth to the tongue

G

G-6-PD deficiency   An enzyme deficiency of the red blood cells, causing hemolytic anemia

Gastric Relating to the stomach

Gastric dilatation Enlargement or dilation of the stomach

Gestation Pregnancy

Glanzmann disease See *Thrombasthenia*

Glasgow Coma Scale A scoring system indicating the severity and projected outcome of head-injured patients, measuring a patient's ocular, verbal, and motor responses to stimulation

Growth arrest The failure or stopping of growth due to illness, injury, or malnutrition

H

Helix A folded rim of cartilage forming the upper part of the anterior surface, the superior surface, and most of the posterior surface of the external ear

Hematoma A localized mass of extravasated blood that is relatively or completely confined within an organ or tissue, a space, or a potential space; the blood is usually clotted (or partly clotted) and, depending on how long it has been there, may manifest various degrees of organization and decolorization

Hemomediastinum An effusion of blood in the mediastinum (see *Mediastinum*)

Hemothorax Blood within the pleural space (see *Pleura*)

Hemotympanum The presence of blood in the middle ear behind the ear drum

Herniation Rupture or protrusion of part of an organ or structure through the wall of the cavity normally containing it

Histological Relating to microscopic anatomy

Humerus The large bone of the upper arm

Hyaloid membrane A membranous thickening forming the capsule of the vitreous within the eye

Hydrocarbon A compound containing only hydrogen and carbon

Hymen A thin crescentic or annular membranous fold, partly occluding the vaginal external orifice in the vagina

Hyperpyrexia Extremely high fever

Hypersensitivity Abnormal sensitivity, usually referring to allergic phenomena

Hypertension High blood pressure

Hypertrophy Overgrowth; increase in bulk

Hyphema Hemorrhage into the anterior chamber of the eye

Hypopharyngeal Relating to the hypopharynx

Hypopharynx The part of the pharynx that lies below the opening of the larynx

Hypovolemic shock Shock caused by loss of blood volume

I

Ileum The third portion of the small intestine, about twelve feet in length, extending from the junction with the jejunum to the ileocecal valve

Immersion burns Burns created by the immersion of body parts in hot water

Immunized Having an immunity produced through medical, and not natural, means

Inflammation A fundamental pathologic process consisting of a dynamic complex of cytologic and histologic reactions that occur in the affected blood vessels and adjacent tissues (of man and other animals) in response to an injury or abnormal stimulation caused by a physical, chemical, or biological agent (or combinations of such agents), including the local reactions and resulting morphological changes, the destruction or removal of the injurious material, and the responses that lead to repair and healing; the so-called cardinal signs of inflammation are redness and heat (or warmth), resulting from an increased amount of blood in the affected tissue that is usually congested; swelling, ordinarily occurring from congestion and exudation; pain, which may result from pressure on (or stretching of) nerve endings, as well as changes in osmotic pressure and pH; disturbance in function, which may result from discomfort of certain movements or the actual destruction of an anatomic part; and occasionally loss of function;

all these signs may be observed in certain instances, but no one of them is necessarily always present

Interhemispheric Between the two hemispheres of the brain

Interspinous ligament A band of fibrous tissue that interconnects spinous processes of adjacent vertebrae

Interstice A small space, gap, or hole in the substance of an organ or tissue

Interstitial Relating to the spaces or interstices in any structure (see *Interstice*)

Intima The inner coat of a blood vessel

Intimal Relating to the intima (see *Intima*)

Intra-abdominal Within the abdomen

Intracranial Within the skull (cranium)

Intraluminal Within a tube or hollow structure

Intraluminal hematoma A hematoma within a tube-shaped structure

Intramural Within the substance of the wall of any cavity or hollow organ

Intraocular Within the eye

Intraoral Within the mouth

Intraperitoneal Within the peritoneal cavity (see *Peritoneal cavity*)

Intrathoracic Within the cavity of the chest

Introitus The entrance into a canal or hollow organ, as the vagina

Ipecac A medication used to induce emesis (vomiting)

J

Jejunum The middle portion of the small intestine, about eight feet in length, between the duodenum and ileum.

L

Laceration A tear, or torn wound

Lateral On or toward the side

Lateral views Side views; X-ray views of the body where the X-ray beam traverses the body from side to side. The right or left side of patient's body is against the film

Ligament A band or sheet of fibrous tissue connecting two or more structures

Ligament of Treitz The suspensory muscle of the duodenum; a flat, broad band of smooth muscle attached to the diaphragm on one end and continuous with the muscular coat of the duodenum on the other, inserting near the junction of the jejunum

Ligamentous support Tissue strength provided by a ligament

Linear Pertaining to or resembling a line

Liver enzymes Enzymes found in the liver (see *Enzyme*)

Liver function studies Measurement of biochemical liver products in the bloodstream that reflect the liver's effectiveness

Livor The discoloration of the skin on the dependent portions of a corpse caused by pooling blood

Lumbar Relating to the part of the back and sides between the rib cage and the pelvis

M

Macula A small orange-yellow spot on the inner surface of the retina at a point corresponding to the posterior pole of the eyeball, and therefore in the visual axis

Macular degeneration A degenerative disease of the retina causing progressive blindness

Magnetic resonance imagery The mapping of the concentration of hydrogen ions in the body by measuring the deexcitation of hydrogen ions caused by passing radiowaves through the body in a strong magnetic field (MRI)

Malaria A protozoal infection of the red blood cells

Malignancy The property or condition of being malignant; virulence; denoting the characteristic of a cancerous growth as distinguished from a benign neoplasm

Malocclusion   Any deviation from a physiologically acceptable contact of opposing teeth

Mandible   The lower jaw bone

Mandibular   Related to the lower jaw

Masque ecchymotique   Skin lesions caused by traumatic asphyxiation

Mediastinal   Related to the mediastinum (see *Mediastinum*)

Mediastinitis   Inflammation of the cellular tissue of the mediastinum

Mediastinum   The median dividing wall of the thoracic cavity, containing the heart, aorta, superior vena cava, trachea, esophagus, thoracic duct, and thymus

Medulla   Soft structure in the center of an organ

Medullary   Pertaining to the medulla (see *Medulla*)

Megaloblastic anemia   An anemia characterized by large number of immature red blood cell forms

Melanoma   A neoplasm arising from cells capable of producing melanin, a skin pigment

Menkes's disease   A hereditary disease involving abnormal absorption of copper

Mesentery   A double layer of peritoneum attached to the abdominal wall and enclosing in its fold a portion or all of one of the abdominal viscera, conveying to it its vessels and nerves. Specifically, the fan-shaped fold of peritoneum encircling the greater part of the small intestines (jejunum and ileum) and attaching it to the posterior abdominal wall

Metaphyseal   Relating to the metaphysis

Metaphyseal fracture   A fracture of the metaphysis of a long bone (see *Metaphysis*)

Metaphyseal injuries   Injuries to the metaphysis (see *Metaphysis*)

Metaphysis   The area of a long bone where the shaft connects to the growth plate near the end of the bone

Metaplasia   The formation of one type of adult tissue by cells that normally produce tissue of another type

Methotrexate A folic acid antagonist used to treat immune disorders and malignancies

Mongolian spots Dark bluish colored birth marks, often found over the sacrum

Mortality Statistically, death rate; the ratio of the number of deaths to a given population in a given situation

Moyamoya disease A nervous system disease characterized by occlusion of the internal carotid artery

MRI Abbreviation for magnetic resonance imagery (see *Magnetic resonance imagery*)

Multifocal Found in multiple locations

Myelodysplasia An occult defect in the spinal column

Myocardial Pertaining to the heart muscle

Myocardium The heart muscle

N

Nasal Relating to the nose

Nasal septum The dividing wall between the two nasal cavities

Neonatal Relating to the period immediately succeeding birth and continuing through the first month of life

Neurological Relating to the nervous system

Neurological examination A physical examination of the nervous system

Neuron The nerve cell and its various processes

Neurosurgical Relating to neurosurgery

O

Occlusion Closing

Occult Hidden, concealed, unsuspected

Occult fracture A condition where there are no clinical signs of a fracture, but a fracture is found on X-ray or bone scan; alternatively, a condition in which there are clinical signs of fracture but no X-ray evidence until after three or four weeks when X-ray shows new bone formation

Ophthalmologist A physician specializing in diseases of the eye

Ophthalmoscopy Examination of the fundus of the eye with an ophthalmoscope

Optic nerve The nerve connecting the retina of the eye to the optic tracts in the brain

Orbit Eye socket

Orofacial Relating to the mouth and face

Oropharynx Relating to the mouth and pharynx

Ossicles The small bones in the inner ear that transmit sound

Ossification The formation and calcification of bone

Osteogenesis imperfecta A family of genetic diseases caused by abnormal collagen formation and metabolism, often causing soft bones that are easily fractured

Osteolysis Absorption and destruction of bony tissue

Osteolytic Pertaining to, characterized by, or causing osteolysis (see *Osteolysis*)

Osteomyelitis Inflammation of the bone marrow, adjacent bone, and epiphysial cartilage

Osteopenia Reduced calcification and reduced density of bones

P

Palate The roof of the mouth

Palpate To examine by feeling and pressing with the palms of the hands and the fingers

Pancreas An abdominal gland that secretes digestive enzymes and insulin

Pancreatic Relating to the pancreas

Pancreatic enzymes Enzymes produced in the pancreas (see *Enzyme*)

Pancreatic pseudocyst An accumulation of fluid in a cyst-like structure in the pancreas, caused by autodigestion of the pancreas by digestive enzymes; pancreatic pseudocysts are often a result of pancreatic trauma

Pancreatitis   Inflammation of the pancreas

Papilledema   Inflammation, edema, and swelling of the optic nerve head

Paralysis   Loss of power of voluntary movement in a muscle

Parietal bone   The bony plate forming the lateral aspect of the skull

Partial thromboplastin time   A laboratory test measuring the clotting ability of blood; the partial thromboplastin time measures thrombin generation in the intrinsic pathway and is a function of all the coagulation factors except factor VII

Pathogenesis   The mode of origin or the development of a disease process

Pathognomonic   Characteristic or indicative of a disease

Pathological fracture   A fracture caused by an underlying disease causing the bone to be unusually fragile

Pathology   Conditions, processes, or results of disease; also, the medical science and specialty practice that deals with all aspects of disease but with special reference to the essential nature, causes, and development of abnormal conditions, as well as the structural and functional changes that result from the disease processes

Pathophysiology   Derangement of function seen in disease; alteration in function as distinguished from structural defects

Penetrating trauma   Injury in which the object causing the trauma pierces and enters the body

Perineum   The area between the thighs extending from the coccyx to the pubis and lying below the pelvic diaphragm

Periorbital   Around the orbit of the eye

Periosteal   Relating to the periosteum (see *Periosteum*)

Periosteum   A thick, fibrous membrane covering the surface of a bone

Petechiae   Minute hemorrhagic spots in the skin, ranging in size from pinpoint to pinhead

Petechial   Relating to petechiae (see *Petechiae*)

Perforation   A small opening in a hollow organ or viscus

Peritoneal cavity The abdominal cavity lined by peritoneum

Peritoneum The serous sac lining the abdominal cavity and covering most of the organs contained therein

Peritonitis Inflammation of the peritoneum

Persistent hyperplastic primary vitreous A congenital eye disease

pH The negative log of the hydrogen ion concentration; a measure of the acidity of blood

Pharyngeal Relating to the pharynx (see *Pharynx*)

Pharynx The upper expanded portion of the digestive tube, between the esophagus below and the mouth and nasal cavities above and in front

Photodocumentation Documenting physical findings with photography or video tape

Platelet An irregularly shaped cellular element in the blood which is necessary for blood coagulation

Platelet count Measurement of the numbers of platelets in the blood

Pleura The membrane enveloping the lungs and lining the walls of the thoracic cavity

Pleural Relating to the pleura (see *Pleura*)

Pleural effusion The escape of fluid from the blood vessels or lymphatics into the pleural cavity

Pneumonia Inflammation of the lungs

Pneumothorax The presence of air in the pleural cavity

Posterior Behind in place; dorsal

Posterior fossa One of three hollow areas on the upper surface on base of the skull, containing the cerebellum

Postmortem After death

Postnatal Occurring after birth

Preretinal hemorrhage Hemorrhages occurring anterior to the retina, beneath the internal limiting membrane

Prevalence The fraction of a group possessing a condition at a given point in time

Prognosis A forecast of the outcome of a disease

Prostaglandin E A naturally occurring lipid substance involved in homeostasis and inflammation, used to treat some types of congenital heart disease in infants

Protein C deficiency A hereditary disease causing thromboembolisms

Prothrombin time A laboratory test measuring the clotting ability of the blood, measuring thrombin generation in the extrinsic pathway and detecting deficiencies in clotting factors II, V, VII, and X, as well as estimating the fibrinogen level

Pulmonary Relating to the lungs

Punctate Points or dots

Purpura Hemorrhages within the skin

Purpura fulminans A severe and usually fatal form of purpura, often caused by bacterial infections

R

Radiograph An X-ray image

Radiological Pertaining to X-rays and other imaging studies used in medicine

Radionuclide bone scans A recording of the distribution of radioactive substances in the body after injection of radioisotopes into the bloodstream (also referred to as a scintigram)

Receptive language The ability to understand language

Respiratory distress The failure of the lungs and the other parts of the respiratory system to work

Resuscitation Restoration of life after apparent death

Retina The inner nervous tunic of the eyeball

Retinal hemorrhage Bleeding into the retina, often associated with head injuries

Retinopathy Noninflammatory degenerative disease of the retina

Retinoschisis Cystic detachment of the retina

Retroperitoneal Behind the peritoneum (see *Peritoneum*)

Retroperitoneal abscess A circumscribed collection of pus behind the peritoneum

Retropharyngeal Behind the pharynx (see *Pharynx*)

Retrospective Looking or directed backward in time

Rickets A deficiency of Vitamin D, causing soft bones

Rocky Mountain spotted fever A tick-born disease caused by the organism *Rickettsia rickettsii*; "tick fever"

S

Sacral Relating to the sacrum (see *Sacrum*)

Sacrum A broad, spade-shaped bone forming the posterior aspect of the pelvis, formed from the fusion of the last five vertebrae; also called the "tailbone"

Sagittal sinus A sinus carrying venous blood in the midline of the brain (see *Venous sinus*)

Scapula The shoulder blade

Scapular Relating to the scapula (see *Scapula*)

Schönlein-Henoch purpura A disease causing bleeding into the skin, and sometimes associated with renal disease or gastrointestinal bleeding

Scurvy A disease caused by a deficiency of Vitamin D, causing, among other things, periosteal elevation of the long bones

Second stage of labor The expulsion of the fetus, from the time of the complete dilation of the cervix to the delivery of the infant

Seizure Convulsion

Serum The fluid portion of the blood obtained after coagulation, distinguished from the circulating plasma in live blood

Serum amylase An enzyme produced in the pancreas that circulates in the blood, elevated levels of which can indicate pancreatic injury or pathology

Serum transaminase levels Measures of enzymes used in the breakdown of proteins, elevated levels of which can be a sign of liver disease

Shaken baby syndrome   A complex pattern of injuries seen in infants who have been violently shaken, often including subdural hematomas and retinal hemorrhages and sometimes fractures of the ribs or long bones

Shear   An injury caused by two oppositely directed parallel forces

Shock   A state of profound mental and physical depression as a consequence of severe physical injury related to inadequate circulation of the blood

Sixth-nerve palsy   Paralysis of the sixth cranial nerve (abducens), causing disorder movement of the eyes and failure of lateral gaze

Skeletal survey   A series of X-rays taken of each bone of the body in cases of suspected child abuse to find unexpected or occult fractures

Soft tissue   Non-bony, non-cartilaginous tissues of the body

Solid organs   Compact, non-fluid organs without interstices or cavities, including in the abdomen the liver, spleen, pancreas, and kidneys

Spinal cord   The elongated portion of the central nervous system contained in the canal of the vertebral column

Spinous   Relating to the spine

Spinous process   A backwards projection from the vertebrae forming the spine or the ridge of the back

Spiral fracture   A fracture encircling the shaft of a long bone caused by a rotational force

Sternal   Relating to the sternum (see *Sternum*)

Sternum   The breastbone

Strabismus   A constant lack of parallelism of the axis of the eyes; "crossed eyes"

Stridor   A high-pitched, noisy respiration, like blowing of the wind

Subacute bacterial endocarditis   A bacterial infection of the valve leaflets of the heart

Subarachnoid hemorrhage   A hemorrhage beneath the arachnoid membrane surrounding the brain

Subconjunctival   Beneath the conjunctiva (see *Conjunctiva*)

Subdural hematoma A hematoma beneath the dura mater, between it and the arachnoid

Subgaleal Beneath the scalp

Subhyaloid On the vitreous side of the hyaloid membrane (see *Hyaloid membrane*)

Subluxation An incomplete dislocation of a joint

Suffocation Impeding respiration; asphyxiation

Suture A fibrous membrane joining two bones of the infant skull

Syphilis A sexually transmitted infectious disease caused by a spirochete, *Treponema pallidum*

Systemic Relating to a system

T

Tactile defensiveness A condition where a person avoids experiencing touch or avoids touching things

Tarsorrhaphy The suturing or pasting together of the eyelid margins

Thermoregulatory control Temperature control of the body

Thoracic Relating to the thorax (see *Thorax*)

Thorax The chest

Thrombasthenia An inherited bleeding disorder where the platelet aggregation is decreased

Thrombocytopenia Decreased number of platelets in the circulating blood

Thrombus A clot occluding a blood vessel

Transection The procedure of cutting across

Transverse fracture A fracture that occurs when the fracture line is at a right angle to the long axis of the bone

Traumatic Caused by wound or injury

Tympanic membrane The eardrum

U

Ultrasonography The delineation of deep or internal structures by measuring the reflection and scattering of ultrasonic waves applied to the body

Umbilical artery The main artery leading from the placenta to the fetus in the uterus

Unmyelinated Nerves not covered with nerve sheaths

Upper gastrointestinal contrast studies Fluoroscopy of the abdomen done after a patient drinks a radiopaque suspension; often referred to as an "upper GI" study, it provides a morphological and functional assessment of the gastrointestinal tract

Urinalysis Analysis of the urine

Urinary tract The tubes that urine passes through, including the kidneys, ureters, bladder, and urethra

Uveitis Inflammation of the uveal tract of the eye, the choroid, ciliary body, and the iris

Uvula A conical projection from the posterior edge of the soft palate

V

Valsalva maneuver The muscular contraction of the chest, abdomen, and diaphragm in forced expiration against a closed glottis that raises the air pressure within the lungs

Vascular Relating to vessels

Vascularity Relating to the quantity of blood vessels

Vasculitis Inflammation of the vessels

Vena cava Large veins carrying blood back to the heart; the inferior vena cava receives blood from the lower extremities and the greater part of the pelvic and abdominal organs, beginning at the level of the fifth lumbar vertebra on the right side, piercing the diaphragm at the level of the eighth thoracic vertebra, and emptying into the back part of the right atrium of the heart; the superior vena cava returns blood from the head and neck, upper extremities, and thorax, formed by union of the two brachiocephalic veins, and also receives the azygos vein

Venous Relating to the veins

Venous sinus   Large blood collection channel formed within the layers of the dura mater

Ventricle   The lower chamber of each half of the heart

Ventricular   Referring to the ventricle (see *Ventricle*)

Vertebra   One of the bony segments of the spinal column

Vertebral   Relating to the vertebrae (see *Vertebra*)

Vertebral disk   A disk interposed between the bodies of adjacent vertebrae

Viscera   Plural of viscus (see *Viscus*)

Viscus   An internal organ, especially one of the large abdominal organs

Vitreous   A transparent, jelly-like substance filling the interior of the eyeball

Von Willebrand's disease   An inherited bleeding disorder characterized by reduced levels of factor VIII and von Willebrand's factor

W

Waldenstrom's macroglobulinemia   A blood disease characterized by excess amounts of macroglobulins (large proteins) in the blood

White matter injuries   Injuries to the white matter, or myelinated neurons, of the brain

Wormian bones   Small, irregular bones found along the sutures of the skull

Z

Zygoma   The bony arch forming the lower, outer portion of the orbit (eye socket)

Reference

Stedman's Medical Dictionary (22nd Ed.). (1972). Baltimore, MD: Williams & Wilkins Co.

Appendix 2

APSAC AMERICAN PROFESSIONAL SOCIETY ON THE ABUSE OF CHILDREN

PRACTICE GUIDELINES

Descriptive Terminology in Child Sexual Abuse Medical Evaluations

INTRODUCTION

The forensic medical evaluation of suspected child sexual abuse victims has developed into a specialized field of practice in the last ten years. Pediatricians, gynecologists, nurse practitioners, and physician assistants may all be called upon to examine children for suspected sexual abuse and describe their findings. The records of such examinations then become medico-legal documents.

Precision in documentation is critical for all who must communicate and understand medical findings. These terminology Guidelines were developed to assist professionals actively involved in the medical diagnosis and treatment of child sexual abuse to establish a shared vocabulary which is clear, precise, and easily communicated. This shared vocabulary will enable those in child protection, law enforcement, and the courts to understand previously confusing and, at times, inconsistent terminology. Consistency in terminology will also assist in the development of a research language.

The terminology presented in these Guidelines emanates primarily from medical dictionary definitions, anatomy texts, and clinicians actively involved in the care of sexually abused children. Unless otherwise noted, definitions are from Stedman's, Ref.1. As experience and scientific knowledge expand, further revision of these guidelines is expected.

ANATOMICAL STRUCTURES

1. ANAL SKIN TAG - A protrusion of anal verge tissue which interrupts the symmetry of the perianal skin folds.

2. ANAL VERGE - The tissue overlying the subcutaneous external anal sphincter at the most distal portion of the anal canal (anoderm) and extending exteriorly to the margin of the anal skin.

3. ANTERIOR COMMISSURE - The union of the two labia minora anteriorly (toward the clitoris).

4. ANUS - The anal orifice, which is the lower opening of the digestive tract, lying in the fold between the buttocks, through which feces are extruded (Ref. 9).

5. CLITORIS - A small cylindrical, erectile body situated at the anterior (superior) portion of the vulva, covered by a sheath of skin called the clitoral hood; homologous with the penis in the male (Ref. 9).

6. FOSSA NAVICULARIS/POSTERIOR FOSSA - Concavity on the lower part of the vestibule situated posteriorly (inferiorly) to the vaginal orifice and extending to the posterior fourchette (posterior commissure).

7. GLANS PENIS - The cap-shaped expansion of the corpus spongiosum at the end of the penis; also called balanus (Ref. 9). It is covered by a mucous membrane and sheathed by the prepuce (foreskin) in uncircumcised males (see Figure 3).

8. GENITALIA (External) - The external sexual organs. In males, includes the penis and scrotum (see Figure 3). In females, includes the contents of the vulva (see Figure 1).

9. HYMEN - This membrane (external vaginal plate or urogenital septum) partially or rarely completely covers the vaginal orifice. This membrane is located at the junction of the vestibular floor and the vaginal canal.

10. LABIA MAJORA - ("outer lips") Rounded folds of skin forming the lateral boundaries of the vulva (see Figure 1).

11. LABIA MINORA - ("inner lips") Longitudinal thin folds of tissue enclosed within the labia majora. In the pubertal child, these folds extend from the clitoral hood to approximately the mid point on the lateral wall of the vestibule. In the adult, they enclose the structures of the vestibule.

12. MEDIAN RAPHE - A ridge or furrow that marks the line of union of the two halves of the perineum (Ref. 9).

13. MONS PUBIS - The rounded, fleshy prominence, created by the underlying fat pad which lies over the symphysis pubis (pubic bone) in the female.

14. PECTINATE/DENTATE LINE - The saw-toothed line of demarcation between the distal (lower) portion of the anal valves and the pectin, the smooth zone of stratified epithelium which extends to the anal verge (Ref. 9). This line is apparent when the external and internal anal sphincters relax and the anus dilates (see Figure 2).

15. PENIS - Male sex organ composed of erectile tissue through which the urethra passes (homologous with the clitoris in the female) (Ref. 9).

16. PERIANAL FOLDS - Wrinkles or folds of the anal verge skin radiating from the anus, which are created by contraction of the external anal sphincter. (Definition not found in Stedman's.)

17. PERINEAL BODY - The central tendon of the perineum located between the vulva and the anus in the female and between the scrotum and anus in the male.

18. PERINEUM - The external surface or base of the perineal body, lying between the vulva and the anus in the female, and the scrotum and the anus in the male (Ref. 1). Underlying the external surface of the perineum is the pelvic floor and its associated structures occupying the pelvic outlet, which is bounded anteriorly by the pubic symphysis (pubic bone), laterally by the ischial tuberosity (pelvic bone) and posteriorly by the coccyx (tail bone).

19. POSTERIOR COMMISSURE - The union of the two labia majora posteriorly (toward the anus).

Descriptive Terminology in Child Sexual Abuse Medical Evaluations **Practice Guidelines**

20. POSTERIOR FOURCHETTE - The junction of two labia minora posteriorly (inferiorly). This area is referred to as a posterior commissure in the prepubertal child, as the labia minora are not completely developed to connect inferiorly until puberty, when it is referred to as the fourchette.

21. SCROTUM - The pouch which contains the testicles and their accessory organs (Ref. 9).

22. URETHRAL ORIFICE - External opening of the canal (urethra) from the bladder.

23. VAGINA - The uterovaginal canal in the female. This internal structure extends from the uterine cervix to the inner aspect of the hymen.

24. VAGINAL VESTIBULE - An anatomic cavity containing the opening of the vagina, the urethra and the ducts of Bartholin's glands. Bordered by the clitoris anteriorly, the labia laterally and the posterior commissure (fourchette) posteriorly (inferiorly). The vestibule encompasses the fossa navicularis immediately posterior (inferior) to the vaginal introitus.

25. VULVA - The external genitalia or pudendum of the female. Includes the clitoris, labia majora, labia minora, vaginal vestibule, urethral orifice, vaginal orifice, hymen, and posterior fourchette (or commissure) (Ref. 9).

HYMENAL MORPHOLOGY (Definitions from Reference 2.)

1. ANNULAR - Circumferential. Hymenal membrane tissue extends completely around the circumference of the entire vaginal orifice.

2. CRIBRIFORM - Hymen with multiple small openings.

3. CRESCENTIC - Hymen with attachments at approximately the 11 and 1 o'clock positions without tissue being present between the two attachments.

4. IMPERFORATE - A hymenal membrane with no opening.

5. SEPTATE - The appearance of the hymenal orifice when it is bisected by a band of hymenal tissue creating two or more orifices.

DESCRIPTIVE TERMS RELATING TO THE HYMEN

1. ESTROGENIZED - Effect of influence by the female sex hormone estrogen resulting in changes to the genitalia. The hymen takes on as a result a thickened, redundant, pale appearance. These changes are observed in neonates, with the onset of puberty and the result of exogenous estrogen.

2. FIMBRIATED/DENTICULAR - Hymen with multiple projections and indentations along the edge, creating a ruffled appearance.

3. NARROW/WIDE HYMENAL RIM - The width of the hymenal membrane as viewed in the coronal plane, i.e., from the edge of the hymen to the muscular portion of the vaginal introitus (see Figure 4).

4. REDUNDANT - Abundant hymenal tissue which tends to fold back on itself or protrude.

5. MEMBRANE THICKNESS - The relative amount of tissue between the internal and external surfaces of the hymenal membrane (see Figure 4).

OTHER STRUCTURES/FINDINGS

1. ACUTE LACERATION - A tear through the full thickness of the skin or other tissue. Examples of lacerations are in Reference 6, page 89 (fourchette); page 113 (hymen); and page 65 (peri-anal tissues).

2. ATTENUATED - This term has been used to describe areas where the hymen is narrow. However, the term should be restricted to indicate a documented change in the width of the posterior portion of the hymen following an injury.

3. DIASTASIS ANI - A congenital midline smooth depression which may be V-shaped or wedge shaped, located either anterior or posterior to the anus, that is due to a failure of fusion of the underlying of the corrugator external anal sphincter muscle (Ref. 5).

4. ERYTHEMA - Redness of tissues.

5. EXTERNAL HYMENAL RIDGE - A midline longitudinal ridge of tissue on the external surface of the hymen. May be either anterior or posterior. Usually extends to the edge of the membrane (Ref. 2).

6. FRIABILITY OF THE POSTERIOR FOURCHETTE/COMMISSURE - A superficial breakdown of the skin in the posterior fourchette (commissure) when gentle traction is applied, causing slight bleeding (Ref. 11).

7. HYMENAL CYST - A fluid-filled elevation of tissue, confined within the hymenal tissue (Ref. 2).

8. HYMENAL CLEFT - An angular or V-shaped indentation on the edge of the hymenal membrane (Ref. 9). When curved, it creates a hollowed or U-shaped depression on the edge of the membrane which has been referred to as a "concavity" (Refs. 10 & 11).

9. LABIAL AGGLUTINATION (labial adhesion) - The result of adherence (fusion) of the adjacent edges of the mucosal surfaces of the labia minora. This may occur at any point along the length of the vestibule although it most commonly occurs posteriorly (inferiorly) (Ref. 6).

10. LINEA VESTIBULARIS - A vertical, pale/avascular line across the posterior fourchette and/or fossa, which may be accentuated by putting lateral traction on the labia major (Refs. 4, 11, & 12).

11. O'CLOCK DESIGNATION - A method by which the location of structures or findings may be designated by using the numerals on the face of a clock. The 12 o'clock position is always superior (up). The 6 o'clock position is always inferior (down). The position of a patient must be indicated when using this designation (see Figure 4).

12. PERINEAL GROOVE - Developmental anomaly, also called "Failure of Midline Fusion" (Ref. 7). This skin and mucosal defect may be located anywhere from the fossa to anus (Ref. 11).

13. PROJECTIONS -

    a. Mound/bump - A solid elevation of hymenal tissue which is wider or as wide as it is long, located on the edge of the hymenal membrane. This structure may be seen at the site where an intravaginal column attaches to the hymen. (Refs. 2, 3, & 11).

b. Hymenal Tag - An elongated projection of tissue rising from any location on the hymenal rim. Commonly found in the midline and may be an extension of a posterior vaginal column (Refs. 6 & 11).

14. SCAR - Fibrous tissue which replaces normal tissue after the healing of a wound (Ref. 6).

15. SYNECHIA - Any adhesion which binds two anatomic structures through the formation of a band of tissue (Ref. 1). A synechia can result in the healing process following an abrasion of tissues.

16. TRANSECTION OF HYMEN (Complete) - A tear or laceration through the entire width of the hymenal membrane extending to (or through its attachment) to the vaginal wall.

17. TRANSECTION OF HYMEN (Partial) - A tear or laceration through a portion of the hymenal membrane not extending to its attachment to the vaginal wall.

18. VAGINAL COLUMNS (columnae rugarum vaginae) - Raised (sagittally oriented) columns most prominent on the anterior wall with less prominence on the posterior wall. May also be observed laterally (Refs. 2 & 3).

19. VAGINAL RUGAE (rugae vaginales) - Folds of epithelium (rugae) running circumferentially from vaginal columns. These rugae account in part for the ability of the vagina to distend (Ref. 11).

20. VASCULARITY (increased) - Dilatation of existing superficial blood vessels.

21. VESTIBULAR BANDS -

a. Periurethral bands - Small bands lateral to the urethra that connect the periurethral tissues to the anterior lateral wall of the vestibule. These bands are usually symmetrical and frequently create a semi-lunar shaped space between the bands on either side of the urethral meatus. Also called urethral supporting ligaments (Ref. 11).

b. Perihymenal bands (pubo vaginal) - Bands lateral to the hymen connecting to the vestibular wall.

DESCRIPTIVE TERMS FOR VARIATIONS IN PERI-ANAL ANATOMY

1. ANAL DILATATION - Opening of the external and internal anal sphincters with minimal traction on the buttocks (Refs. 5 & 6).

2. ANAL FISSURE - A superficial break (split) in the perianal skin which radiates out from the anal orifice (Refs. 6 &11).

3. FLATTENED ANAL FOLDS - A reduction or absence of the perianal folds or wrinkles, noted when the external anal sphincter is partially or completely relaxed.

4. VENOUS CONGESTION - Pooling of venous blood in the peri-anal tissues resulting in a purple discoloration which may be localized or diffuse (Ref. 6).

FIGURE 1.

ANATOMIC STRUCTURES IN THE PREPUBERTAL GIRL

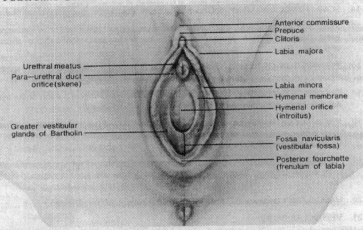

Anterior commissure
Prepuce
Clitoris
Labia majora

Urethral meatus
Para—urethral duct orifice (skene)

Labia minora
Hymenal membrane
Hymenal orifice (introitus)

Greater vestibular glands of Bartholin

Fossa navicularis (vestibular fossa)
Posterior fourchette (frenulum of labia)

Reprinted with permission from Finkel M; DeJong AR: Medical findings in child sexual abuse. In Reece RM: Child Abuse, Medical Diagnosis and Management. Lea & Febiger, Philadelphia, 1994, p. 210.

FIGURE 2.

CROSS-SECTIONAL VIEW OF THE ANUS

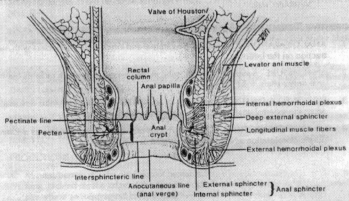

Valve of Houston

Rectal column
Anal papilla

Levator ani muscle

Internal hemorrhoidal plexus
Deep external sphincter
Longitudinal muscle fibers

Pectinate line
Pecten

Anal crypt

External hemorrhoidal plexus

Intersphincteric line
Anocutaneous line (anal verge)
External sphincter
Internal sphincter
} Anal sphincter

Reprinted with permission from Giardino AP; Finkel M; Giardino ER; Seidl T; Ludwig S: A Practical Guide to the Evaluation of Sexual Abuse in the Prepubertal Child., Sage Publications, Newbury Park, CA, 1992, p. 50.

Descriptive Terminology in Child Sexual Abuse Medical Evaluations **Practice Guidelines**

FIGURE 3.

PREPUBERTAL MALE GENITALIA (CIRCUMCISED)

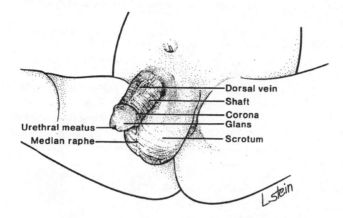

Reprinted with permission from Giardino AP; Finkel M; Giardino ER; Seidl T; Ludwig S: A Practical Guide to the Evaluation of Sexual Abuse in the Prepubertal Child. Sage Publications, Newbury Park, CA, 1992, p. 33.

FIGURE 4.

FRONTAL AND CROSS-SECTIONAL VIEWS OF HYMEN, PATIENT SUPINE

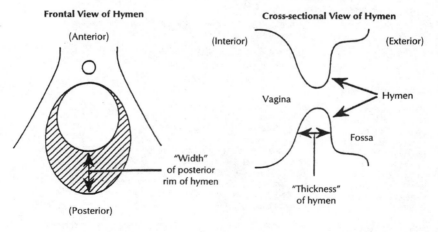

Descriptive Terminology in Child Sexual Abuse Medical Evaluations **Practice Guidelines**

REFERENCES

1. Stedman's Medical Dictionary, 22nd Edition, Williams & Wilkins Co., Baltimore, 1972.

2. Berenson A; Heger A; Andrews S: Appearance of the hymen in newborns. Pediatrics, 1991; 87:458-465.

3. Berenson AB; Heger AH; Hayes JM; Bailey RK; Emans SJ: Appearance of the hymen in prepubertal girls. Pediatrics, 1992: 89:387-394.

4. McCann J; Wells R; Simon M; Voris J: Genital findings in prepubertal children selected for non-abuse: A descriptive study. Pediatrics, 1990; 86:428-439.

5. McCann J; Voris J; Simon M; Wells R: Perianal findings in prepubertal children selected for non-abuse: A descriptive study. Child Abuse & neglect, 1989; 12:179-193.

6. Chadwick D; Berkowitz CD; Kerns D; McCann J; Reinhart MA; Strickland S: Color Atlas of Child Sexual Abuse, 1989. Yearbook Medical Publishers, Chicago.

7. McCann J: Use of the colposcope in childhood sexual abuse examination. Ped Clin N Amer, 1990; 37: 863-880.

8. Adams JA; Phillips P; Ahmad M: The usefulness of colposcopic photographs in the evaluation of suspected child abuse. Adol Pediatr Gynecol, 1990; 3:75-82.

9. Dorland's Illustrated Medical Dictionary, 27th Edition, W.B. Saunders Co., Philadelphia, 1988.

10. Kerns DL; Ritter ML; Thomas RG: Concave hymenal variations in suspected child sexual abuse. Pediatrics, 1992; 90:265-272.

11. Heger A; Emans SJ: Evaluation of the Sexually Abused Child, A Medical Textbook and Photographic Atlas. Oxford University Press, 1992.

12. Kellog ND; Parra JM: Linea vestibularis: A previously undescribed normal genital structure in female neonates. Pediatrics, 1991; 87:926-929.

13. Giardino AP; Finkel M; Giardino ER; Seidl T; Ludwig S: A Practical Guide to the Evaluation of Sexual Abuse in the Prepubertal Child. Sage Publications, Newbury Park, CA, 1992.

14. Finkel M; DeJong AR: Medical findings in child sexual abuse. In Reece RM: Child Abuse, Medical Diagnosis and Management. Lea & Febiger, Philadelphia, 1994.

ACKNOWLEDGEMENTS

These guidelines were produced by the Terminology Subcommittee of the APSAC Task Force on Medical Evaluation of Suspected Child Abuse. The Terminology Subcommittee is chaired by Joyce Adams, MD. The Terminology Subcommittee held open meetings at the San Diego Conference on Responding to Child Maltreatment in January of 1991, 1992, 1993, and 1995 to review and reach consensus on the terms listed. Active members of the subcommittee include Martin Finkel, DO; Mary Gibbons, MD; Marcia Herman-Giddens, PA, DrPH; Susan Horowitz, MD; John McCann, MD; Margaret Moody, MD; David Muram, MD; Sue Perdew, RN, Ph.D.; Sue Ross,RN, PNP; Sara Schuh, MD; Rizwan Shah, MD; and Elizabeth Young, MD. Valuable contributions were also made by Carol Berkowitz, MD; S. Jean Emans, MD; Dirk Huyer, MD; Carole Jenny, MD, MBA; and Susan Pokorny, MD.

About the Author

Carole Jenny, M.D., is Director of the Child Advocacy and Protection Team at The Children's Hospital, Denver, Colorado, and is Associate Professor of Pediatrics at the University of Colorado School of Medicine. She also directs medical programs at the C. Henry Kempe National Center for the Prevention and Treatment of Child Abuse and Neglect. Prior to coming to Denver, she was Medical Director of the Harborview Sexual Assualt Center in Seattle, Washington, and was on the faculty of the School of Medicine at the University of Washington. She attended the University of Missouri, Dartmouth Medical School, and the University of Washington. She was an intern in pediatrics at the University of Colorado and a resident at the Children's Hospital of Philadelphia. After her residency, she was a Robert Wood Johnson Clinical Scholar at the University of Pennsylvania and received an MBA in Health Care degree from the Wharton School. Her research interests include sexually transmitted diseases, head trauma in infants, and the use of colposcopy in the evaluation of sexual abuse and assault. She recently served on the Board of Directors of the American Professional Society on the Abuse of Children and is Chair of the Executive Committee of the Section on Child Abuse and Neglect of the American Academy of Pediatrics.

Medical Evaluation of
Physically and Sexually Abused Children
Checklist for Continuing Education Credits

To be eligible to receive 6 CE credits for this program, the following must be completed and returned to the following address:

PsychoEducational Resources
P.O. Box 2196
Keystone Heights, FL 32656

—— A completed knowledge test

—— A completed "Client Vignette" form

—— A signed statement (below) verifying your completion of this home study program

—— A completed program evaluation/participant satisfaction form (see below)

Your name as you want it to appear on your CE certificate: _____

Address: _____ Degree:_____

_____ Discipline: _____

_____ Date: _____

I confirm that I personally have completed the above test, and I am submitting it for CE certification.

Signature: _____

Evaluation of Program

Please circle the appropriate response to each of the items below. Your feedback will be used by PER to evaluate the appropriateness of this form of home study as a Continuing Education activity and will provide guidance in the selection and development of future offerings in the video series.

	Strongly Agree		Neutral		Strongly Disagree
The content of the program was informative for a professional at my level of training.	1	2	3	4	5
The material included in this program was appropriate to my learning objectives.	1	2	3	4	5
The questions comprising the CE quiz fairly tested my knowledge of the program materials.	1	2	3	4	5
I would be interested in participating in similar CE offerings in the future.	1	2	3	4	5

Estimate of amount of time required for study of all materials and completion of CE tests: _____

Suggestions for future topics:

Medical Evaluation of Physically and Sexually Abused Children

KNOWLEDGE TEST

To be eligible to receive 6 Continuing Education credits for this home study module, please complete the knowledge test below, circling the correct response to each item. You must respond correctly to at least 80% of the items to pass.

1. Which of the following is not true of children who die due to either neglect or abuse?

    a. The rate of child abuse fatalities rose over 50% from 1985 to 1991.

    b. Approximately 10% of children who died from either neglect or abuse had prior or current contact with child protective services.

    c. Approximately 55% of the children who died were under age one.

    d. Approximately 20% of the children who died were over age five.

2. Studies suggest that there are a number of risk factors associated with child abuse and injury. All of the following are risk factors except:

    a. gender of the child

    b. whether or not the child is a member of a minority

    c. maternal education and employment

    d. paternal marital status

3. When discussing the need to gather a complete medical history of the allegedly abused child, Carole Jenny, M.D., notes that:

    a. A history from the child, if the child is verbal, can be helpful and should be gathered without the presence of a parent if possible.

    b. A history from the child is often helpful and should always be conducted in the presence of a parent.

    c. A history from the child can be helpful but should always be gathered in the presence of a neutral third-party and an attorney representing the facility.

    d. Gathering complete medical histories from children is never called for since they are frequently unreliable.

4. When conducting physical examinations of allegedly abused children, it is best to:

    a. conduct the examination as soon as possible, even if the child is not medically stable.

    b. avoid referencing other medical records since this might "tip your hand" to the child's parents.

    c. examine other children at risk in the household.

    d. limit your examination to nongenital areas to avoid contaminating possible evidence.

5. Which of the following imaging techniques would be most helpful in detecting child abuse-related head injuries?

   a. X-ray

   b. MRI

   c. CT

   d. Ultrasound

6. Which of the following is not an element to be included in the medical chart documentation of suspected child abuse?

   a. a history of the injury

   b. a description of the injury

   c. an affidavit from the parent or caretaker describing their response once they became aware of the injury

   d. an analysis of whether the injury fit the history given

7. Photodocumentation of injuries is considered:

   a. an important part of the chart documentation process.

   b. an unimportant part of the documentation process since photos are inadmissible evidence in criminal proceedings.

   c. not as helpful as accurately drawn pictures of the injury.

   d. a potentially harmful invasion of the child's privacy.

8. Certain injuries are more common in cases of abuse than in accidents. In the case of abdominal injuries, which of the following is correct?

   a. Those resulting from abuse are less commonly fatal than those resulting from accidents because the former involve the use of less force.

   b. For a variety of reasons, children are more susceptible to abdominal trauma than adults.

   c. Such injuries typically co-occur with bowel injuries.

   d. Injuries to spleen and kidneys are common in abuse cases.

9. Some authors, when studying the prevalence rate of abdominal injuries in children, suggest that _____ injuries are more common than recognized in abused children.

   a. pancreatic

   b. spleen

   c. kidney

   d. liver

10. Ultrasound is *not* the recommended imaging technique for _____ injuries.

   a. pancreatic

   b. kidney

   c. duodenal

   d. chest

11. Jenny points out that tap water immersion burns share all of the following characteristics *except* that they
    a. have no clear "tide mark."
    b. have no splash marks.
    c. are most commonly found on the hands and feet.
    d. are more likely to be "bilateral."

12. Liquid grease burns are particularly damaging because of the ability of grease to adhere to the skin. If you suspected such a burn had occurred, one tell-tale sign would be:
    a. the presence of irregular edges at the burn site.
    b. the presence of "unilateral" burns.
    c. the burn would be worse at the point of initial contact.
    d. the burn would form a crescent shape in the skin.

13. The most common cause of heat stroke is:
    a. placing the child in a small room with a space heater.
    b. allowing the child to remain outside during the summer without access to fluids.
    c. leaving the child in a parked car.
    d. allowing the child to play around a fireplace.

14. The two most predictive factors for diagnosing burn abuse are treatment delay and
    a. burns attributed to a sibling.
    b. different historical accounts of the injury.
    c. inappropriate parental affect.
    d. an injury inconsistent with the history given.

15. Studies suggest that children with abusive burn injuries have higher rates of _____ than children with accidental burns.
    a. depression
    b. anxiety
    c. tic-type disorders
    d. conduct disorders

16. The compliance and flexibility of a child's chest means that:
    a. Chest injuries are particularly dangerous for young children.
    b. Chest injuries are seldom dangerous for young children.
    c. Chest injuries are rarely recognized as a result of child abuse.
    d. Children are more likely than adults to survive accidents.

17. Injuries to the lips are not uncommon in children between what ages?

    a. 0-6 months

    b. 6-18 months

    c. 18-36 months

    d. Injuries to the lips of young children are uncommon regardless of age and often suggest child abuse.

18. According to Jenny, which of the following types of fractures are almost always associated with child abuse?

    a. posterior rib fractures

    b. scapular fractures

    c. metaphyseal fractures

    d. fractures of the diaphysis of the long bones

19. Abuse is most likely to be the case when children:

    a. complain of frequent headaches.

    b. have more than one unexplained fracture.

    c. bond most closely with their mothers.

    d. have difficulty initiating sleep.

20. Based upon recommendations from the American Academy of Pediatrics, pediatric "body grams" _____ are "unacceptable."

    a. on a single X-ray film

    b. using CT

    c. using MRI

    d. regardless of the imaging technique

21. Skeletal surveys are mandatory in all cases of suspected abuse in children:

    a. under age 2.

    b. between 4 and 8.

    c. after age 10.

    d. of all ages.

22. All of the following are factors that make young infants more vulnerable to head injury by shaking *except:*

    a. The infant brain is smaller than a more mature brain.

    b. The infant brain is harder than a more mature brain.

    c. The infant brain is surrounded by more cerebrospinal fluid than a more mature brain.

    d. The infant's large head is poorly supported by weak neck muscles.

23. Which of the following is not true of skull fractures resulting from abusive head trauma?

    a. They are more likely to be multiple.

    b. They are more likely to be complex.

    c. They are more likely to be depressed.

    d. They are more likely to be narrow.

24. When examining a child for suspected child abuse, and based upon your knowledge that subdural hematomas frequently accompany abuse, which of the following imaging techniques would it be important to use?

    a. X-ray

    b. CT

    c. MRI

    d. PET

25. An 18-month-old child is presented suffering from retinal hemorrhages. According to Jenny, this presentation:

    a. means little in the absence of further information.

    b. should be considered to be caused by child abuse.

    c. is frequent in children less than two years of age.

    d. suggests that the child has recently been involved in a high-speed car accident.

26. Which of the following is *not* one of the special conditions outlined by Jenny when considering whether or not retinal hemorrhages are caused by abuse?

    a. Retinal hemorrhages are commonly found in newborns after delivery.

    b. High altitude can cause retinal hemorrhages.

    c. Retinal hemorrhages may result from the child attempting to lift an object more than twice his/her weight.

    d. Efforts to resuscitate the child can cause retinal hemorrhages.

27. At least one study found that abused children, compared to nonabused children, had

    a. more injuries to the head and face.

    b. more injuries to the back and neck.

    c. approximately the same number and types of injuries.

    d. fewer, but more severe, injuries.

28. Multiple bruises of different ages suggest:

    a. that the child has been abused by many different people.

    b. that various instruments of abuse have been used.

    c. ongoing abuse.

    d. In the absence of more information, multiple bruises of different ages are not suggestive of abuse.

29. In cases of abuse, which of the following is *not* one of the types of abrasions that Jenny suggests may occur in cases of abuse?
    a. impact
    b. brush
    c. pattern
    d. spiral

30. Jenny notes that some folk medicine practices can cause lesions that may be confused with abuse. An example is _____, which involves burning herbs on the skin to rid the child of illness.
    a. *cao gio*
    b. moxibustion
    c. pica
    d. frotteurism

31. Which of the following is not considered to be an identifiable risk factor for sexual abuse?
    a. race and social class
    b. gender
    c. age
    d. social isolation of family

32. When performing a medical examination of a child who is believed to have been sexually abused, it is best to conduct that examination within _____ hours at a(n) _____.
    a. 24, hospital emergency room
    b. 72, hospital emergency room
    c. 72, outpatient clinic/doctor's office
    d. 48, outpatient clinic/doctor's office

33. According to Jenny, many of the behavioral signs of sexual abuse are similar to children who suffer from _____.
    a. Attention Deficit/Hyperactivity Disorder (ADHD)
    b. Posttraumatic Stress Disorder (PTSD)
    c. Rett's Disorder
    d. Separation Anxiety Disorder (SAD)

34. Which of the following behaviors would suggest that the child has been sexually abused?
    a. masturbation
    b. "playing house"
    c. touching one's own sexual organs
    d. overt imitation of sexual acts

35. Because of the "medical-legal" implications of interviewing an allegedly sexually abused child, Jenny stresses the use of
    a. "yes/no" questions.
    b. non-leading questions.
    c. open-ended questions.
    d. questions tailored to the child's developmental level.

36. Regarding the medical interview of an allegedly sexually abused child, Jenny suggests that interviews be:
    a. observed through a "one-way" mirror.
    b. audiotaped.
    c. audio or videotaped with the permission of the parents.
    d. recorded only after consulting with social service agencies

37. The major disadvantage to using a photocolposcope in case of sexual abuse is:
    a. cost.
    b. possible re-traumatization of the child.
    c. exposing the child to a painful procedure.
    d. that this procedure is not admissible as evidence in court.

38. All of the following are important to maintaining the chain of custody regarding evidence in cases of alleged sexual abuse except:
    a. collection of evidence.
    b. handling of evidence.
    c. preservation of evidence in freezers with temperatures above –10 degrees Celsius.
    d. storage of evidence.

39. When recording a child's history of sexual and/or physical abuse for the medical record, it is best to:
    a. use vague, non-specific terms to protect the privacy of the child.
    b. use direct quotes.
    c. not record the questions asked of the child.
    d. have a parent or guardian present during the questioning.

40. According to the American Academy of Pediatrics, the presence of _____ is a definite indication of sexual abuse requiring reporting:
    a. a positive culture for gonorrhea
    b. chlamydia trachomatis
    c. herpes virus infections
    d. trachomonas vaginalis

The following clinical vignette is designed to help you "think through" your assessment of a suspected case of child abuse, integrating the information you have just studied in the accompanying learning guide. To receive CE credit for this program, you must complete and return these short essay questions with the Knowledge Test and evaluation form.

CLINICAL VIGNETTE

A 6-year-old Caucasian female is brought by her mother to the Emergency Room where you work for the treatment of an apparently accidental burn on the child's left foot. The mother gives a very precise accounting of the accident and appears to have sought treatment in a timely manner. The mother seems truly concerned about the well-being of her daughter. (Attach additional pages as needed for responses to Client Vignette questions.)

CLINICAL VIGNETTE: QUESTION 1

1. Based on the risk factors discussed by Jenny, to what extent should you be concerned about the possibility of abuse based on these facts?

2. Upon examining the burn, you notice that it is a partial thickness burn, and that it appears to be bilateral and lacks a splash mark. By this time the child's father has arrived and you begin to ask him about the accident. His account of the event differs markedly from that of the mother. What would you do at this point?

3. Discuss the key elements of your approach to interviewing the child concerning possible abuse. How would you proceed with this interview?